MILLER'S
GLASS
Antiques Checklist

Consultant: Mark West

General Editors:
Judith and Martin Miller

MILLER'S

MILLER'S ANTIQUES CHECKLIST: GLASS

Consultant: Mark West

First published in Great Britain in 1994 by Miller's
an imprint of Reed Consumer Books Limited
Michelin House,
81 Fulham Road
London SW3 6RB
and Auckland, Melbourne, Singapore and Toronto

Series Editor	Alison Starling
Editor	Katie Piper
Contributing Editor	Janet Gleeson
Indexer	Hilary Bird
Art Editor	Geoff Fennell
Illustrator	Simon Miller
Special Photography	Ian Booth
Production	Heather O'Connell

A CIP catalogue record for this book is available
from the British Library

ISBN 1 85732 271 1

Set in Caslon 540, Caslon 224 bold and Caslon 3
Origination and printing by Mandarin Offset
Printed in Malaysia

cover picture: *An overlay wine jug, Stourbridge, c.1869*
picture on p.1: *A white-on-green overlay vase, c.1860*

Two cameo bottle vases *(left) Japanese-style vase by Stevens & Williams, c.1885, (right) three-colour cameo by Thomas Webb & Sons, c.1885*

CONTENTS

BRITISH AND IRISH DECANTERS

ENGLISH AND IRISH CUT GLASS

GLASS LIGHTING

19THC BRITISH GLASS

GLOSSARY 176

SELECTED DESIGNERS AND MANUFACTURERS 178

BIBLIOGRAPHY 185

INDEX 186

PICTURE CREDITS AND ACKNOWLEDGEMENTS 192

HOW TO USE THIS BOOK

When I first started collecting antiques although there were many informative books on the subject I still felt hesitant when it came to actually buying an antique. What I really wanted to do was interrogate the piece – to find out what it was and whether it was genuine.

The *Glass* Checklist will show you how to assess a piece as an expert would, and provides checklists of questions you should ask before making a purchase. The answer to most (if not all) of the questions should be "yes", but remember there are always exceptions to the rule: if in doubt, seek expert guidance.

The book is divided into collecting categories, including cut glass, decanters, and 18thC English drinking glasses. It looks as the work of craftsmen from Britain, Europe and the United States, and studies all the main glassmaking techniques. At the back of the book are a glossary, bibliography and a list of principal makers and designers, and their marks.

Treat the book as a knowledgeable companion, and soon you will find that antique collecting is a matter of experience, and of knowing how to ask the right questions.

JUDITH MILLER

Each double-page spread looks at items belonging to a particular category of collecting.

The first page shows a carefully-chosen representative item of a type that can usually be found at antiques stores or auction houses (rather than only in museums).

The caption gives the date and dimensions of the piece shown, and a code for the price range of this type of article.

A checklist of questions gives you the key to recognizing, dating and authenticating antique pieces of the type shown.

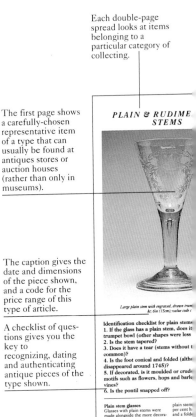

PLAIN & RUDIME[NT] STEMS

Large plain stem with engraved, drawn trum[pet] ht; 6in (15cm); value code c

Identification checklist for plain stems
1. If the glass has a plain stem, does it [have a] trumpet bowl (other shapes were less [common])
2. Is the stem tapered?
3. Does it have a tear (stems without t[ears are] common)?
4. Is the foot conical and folded (altho[ugh it] disappeared around 1745)?
5. If decorated, is it moulded or crude[ly cut with] motifs such as flowers, hops and barle[y or] vines?
6. Is the pontil snapped off?

Plain stem glasses
Glasses with plain stems were made alongside the more decorative balustroid between 1730 and 1760; they were less expensive and designed for everyday use. The glass in the main picture shows the typical features of a plain stem [...] per cent h[...] and a folde[...] protect ag[...] (although [...] after 1745 [...] ture was a [...] tear, usual[...]

88

VALUE CODES
Throughout this book, the caption of the piece in the main picture is followed by a letter which corresponds to the approximate value (at the time of printing) of that piece. The values should be used only as a general guide. The dollar/sterling conversion has been made at a rate of £1=US $1.50; in the event of a change in rate, adjust the dollar value accordingly.

Useful background information is provided about the craftsman, factory or type of ware.

The second page shows you what details to look for.

stems with a drawn bowl shape were made in two pieces, those with other bowl shapes were generally made in three pieces, with a join visible between the base of the bowl and the stem.

This dwarf ale glass c.1770, has been "half-wrythen". Others are engraved with hops and barley.

Jellies
Foods such as calf's foot jelly, savoury and other jellies, were popular during the 18thC. the glasses they were eaten from have come to known as "jellies".

Information helps you to detect fakes, copies and reproductions.

This rare plain stem mead glass shows the distinctive cup-shaped bowl peculiar to mead glass. Plain stems were also used for wine and beer.
* Decoration on plain stems included engraving (fruiting vines, flowers, hops and barley) and moulded patterns.

Rudimentary stems
Throughout the 18thC many small glasses were made with very short stems, or bowls set directly on the foot. Known as rudimentary stems, they were less expensive glasses, made for taverns and everyday use.

This typical plain jelly has a flared rim and a short stem with a bladed knop. The bowls are usually about 4in (10.2cm) high, and frequently-found shapes include, pan-topped, bell, round funnel, cup, and sometimes hexagonal. The most common form of decoration is moulding to the bowl, and some jellies have handles.
* If a jelly has only one handle it is possible that the second has been lost: look out for recutting.

Further photographs show:
* items in a similar style by the same craftsman or factory
* similar, but perhaps less valuable wares that may be mistaken for the more collectable type
* common variations on the piece shown in the main picture
* similar wares by other craftsmen
* the range of shapes or decorative motifs associated with a particular factory or period.

Ale glasses were made with rudimentary stems of all types. They are usually 4–5in (10.2 x 12.7cm) tall and always have conical bowls. There are two main forms of decoration: "wrythen" moulding was formed by twisting vertical ribs to give a spiral effect.

Drams are found with all 18thC stem forms, and were generally small, inexpensive glasses used in taverns to serve spirits such as gin and brandy. Bowl shapes vary enormously – this dram has an barrel bowl, stems are short and simple, and they have conical feet which were folded before 1750, and may be uneven.
* Forms of decoration include crude engraving, moulding on the bowl and knopped stems.

89

Hints and tips help you to assess factors that affect value – for example, condition and availability.

Marks, signatures and serial numbers are explained.

The codes are as follows:

A £10,000+ ($15,000+)
B £5-10,000 ($7,500-15,000)
C £2-5,000 ($3-7,500)
D £1-2,000 ($1,500-2,000)

E £500-1,000 ($750-1,000)
F £200-500 ($300-750)
G £100-200 ($150-200)
H under £100 ($150)

INTRODUCTION

Glass is one the few areas of antiques collecting where items are still relatively undervalued, unlike silver or porcelain. Indeed, some antique glass wares, such as 18th and 19thC decanters, may cost only as much as a good quality modern equivalent. For someone keen to make an investment, it is interesting to know that while a new decanter will be worth about one tenth of its cost price once the purchase has been made, an antique will hold its value and may even appreciate over time.

This book covers most important areas of antique glass collecting, and follows the history of the subject from the evolution of glass production in ancient times, to the highly innovative techniques of the 19thC. Also examined are techniques, forms and styles from glassmaking centres all over the world, such as Britain, the United States, Germany, France, Italy, Spain, the Netherlands, Scandinavia, Russia, India, China and Japan. Emphasis has been placed, however, on groups of items that are more accessible to the amateur collector, including decanters, cut glass, 18thC English drinking glasses and 19thC glass. Pieces from these categories are both interesting and relatively affordable.

Within the field of antique glass collecting there is a huge variety of areas in which to specialize: a look at the different glassmaking centres is an interesting way to start. Glass from mainland Europe offers an enormous selection, ranging from medieval German glass to early Venetian items. More easily available are 18th and 19thC pieces which include beautiful coloured and engraved glass from old regions of central Europe including Bohemia, Saxony, Potsdam and Silesia.

French glass made before the mid-18thC is not widely available. However, after the establishment of the major glass houses – Baccarat, St. Louis and Clichy – beautiful wares of the highest quality were produced in France. Paperweights made by these factories, although expensive are regarded as works of art and are extremely collectable.

American glass, while a relatively recent phenomenon, is also widely collected, ranging from pieces of lacy glass by the Boston & Sandwich Glass Co., to Tiffany's famous lamps and other art glass. A number of important paperweights were also produced by the main American firms.

The focus for collecting English glass is mainly based around drinking glasses and decanters from the 18thC. Glasses made throughout the century are characterized by distinctive stem forms that act as a guide to the date of production. The evolution of the shape of decanters and other serving bottles has also been well-documented and individual items offer a tangible account of the development of glassmaking during this period.

The glass industry in Ireland expanded rapidly in the late 18thC because glass production in England became so heavily taxed, and many English companies established factories in Ireland. The country became famous for high quality, cut lead crystal glass. Bowls, jugs, dishes and decanters were all produced in an elegant, heavily-cut style that has become known as "Anglo-Irish". Excise taxes were extended to include Ireland in 1825 which sent the industry into decline, but following the repeal of the taxes in both England and Ireland in 1845, glassmaking thrived once again.

19thC glass is characterized by innovation and experimentation. Glass made in Britain during the Victorian era (1837–1901), for example, shows glassmakers testing their techniques and decorative skills to the limits. Coloured glass is one interesting area: uranium, now known to be a highly dangerous material, was used to create a variety of effects, including a yellow-green glass which changed through pink to red when re-heated.

The question of how to display a collection of glass is one that needs to be given a great deal of thought. Obviously security is a major concern, but many lockable cabinets are often too dark to show items off to their best advantage. Cabinets with doors, while enabling a collection to be locked away, also help to keep dust away from the glass. The appearance of glass is most effective when presented on a clear glass shelf that allows light to pass through the item. Glass is enhanced by lighting either from directly above or below, and also serves to minimize shadows and reflection. Remember that although a bright light will emphasize colour, it may obscure the tone and shape of a piece.

Giving advice on buying is always difficult. Antique glass is rarely marked, and while reading the wide variety of literature available makes an excellent starting point, the only way to gain a real understanding is to handle the items themselves. Most specialist dealers will be pleased to talk you through their stock, and are a useful source of information. The larger auction houses hold viewing sessions during the week prior to a sale, and are helpful even if one has no intention of buying, because it is often possible to handle the items. Large auction houses are a highly reliable source for collectors, and make every effort to ensure that everything sold is genuine and correctly described. Smaller sales, collector's fairs and markets are less reliable places to buy, so think seriously before making a purchase. They can, however, be good places to look, handle and learn, and bargains are not uncommon.

A specialist dealer may not be the least expensive place to buy antique glass, but will always sell items that are, to his or her knowledge, genuine. Items can be returned if damaged or misrepresented and money refunded. Some dealers will even trade back a piece at a later date: if reputable, a dealer will never be embarrassed about buying back stock.

To conclude, the best way to collect antique glass is by aiming for top quality and condition, rather than quantity. It is tempting to amass a large number of less expensive pieces when starting out, but it is more rewarding in the long run, both from a collector's and a financial point of view, to buy a single, good quality piece using a similar amount of money.

BASICS

Glass is probably one of the most important, and yet one of the most over-looked materials used in every-day life. By its nature, glass is usually colourless and transparent, so that we see only what lies inside or beyond it: when observing a view through a window, few people actually look at the window pane itself, when switching on an electric light, we rarely consider the glass used to make the bulb.

Decorative and functional glass items have been made for thousands of years and make a very exciting area in which to collect: each piece gives an impression of the social, political and economic climate in which it was made.

Every potential collector of antique glass must know something about the following:
* the material itself
* the different forms of glass that have been used over the centuries
* the different ways of shaping glass
* the methods of colouring glass
* decorative techniques
* how to judge authenticity
* how to care for a collection.

GLASS
The body of a glass item is technically known as "metal"; this also helps to avoid confusing glass as an item (a drinking glass), and glass as a material. The colour and texture of the metal will vary according to the ingredients used.

Ingredients
The basic component of glass is silica, a substance that makes up nearly 75 per cent of the Earth's surface, and is most commonly found in the form of flint, quartz or sand. Silica is the most variable component of the mix. Coastal sand, although the most widely available, is not the most refined form of silica and will often contain impurities such as metal deposits which discolour the resulting glass: the tints in early glass can act as a guide to the area of manufacture. Most sand intended for glass production today is carefully sorted and graded. On its own, silica will melt only at a very high temperature. The addition of an alkaline flux helps to bind the ingredients together, and will also reduce the melting point of the mix.

Water-glass
When silica is mixed with sodium carbonate only, water-glass is produced. While similar to glass in appearance, it is soluble in water.

Soda glass
An early metal, soda glass is produced by super-heating (to a temperature of over 1000°C) a mixture of silica, sodium carbonate and calcium carbonate (in the form of chalk or limestone). Because this form of glass is relatively simple to produce, soda glass is still used today to make bottles, and other less expensive, disposable glass items.

The production of clear glass, designed to imitate the mineral rock crystal, has always been a glassmaker's goal: the Romans made *cristallum*, and the early Venetians manufactured *vetro di cristallo* (glass of crystal) using soda derived from burnt seaweed.

Potash glass
Potash glass was first made in Bohemia in northern Europe. Potash, or potassium carbonate was made by burning wood and bracken from the Bohemian forests, hence the German name for potash glass is *waldglas* ("forest glass"). Potash glass is hard, and is unsuitable for cutting.

Lead crystal
In 1671 George Ravenscroft, a British glassmaker, discovered a "particular sort of Christaline Glasse", that he called "glass of lead". This form of metal, made using a high proportion of lead oxide in the mix, was a relatively soft, brilliant glass that was highly suitable for cut and engraved decoration. The proportions of the ingredients have changed slightly since the 17thC, but remain basically the same: three parts silica, two parts red lead, one part potash, and a little salt-petre, borax and arsenic.

SHAPING GLASS
Ancient glass was made by winding threads of molten glass around a core made from sand or clay. Once the core was covered, the vessel was "marvered" or smoothed on a flat surface to fuse the threads together and make a solid item. The core was then removed. This technique was known as *core forming*.

Blown glass
* *Free-blown* glass, invented by the Romans in the 1stC BC, is formed from a blob of molten glass, a *gather*, that is placed on a hollow, iron blowing rod. Once the main body has been formed it is often transferred to a second, pontil rod, for further shaping and manipulation. On early pieces, the pontil rod was simply "snapped off" from the base leaving a rough pontil mark.
* *Mould-blown* glass is created by blowing the gather into a wooden (later a metal) mould made up of one or more parts.

Pressed glass
In the early 19thC a technique known as *press-moulding* was introduced, which involved pouring molten glass into a mould, and forcing the glass into all parts of the mould using a plunger.

This technique was mechanized in the United States in the 19thC, and controlled, compressed air was used to push the plunger into the mould.

COLOURED GLASS
Glass can be coloured in a number of ways:
* the entire glass batch can be coloured by the addition of a metal oxide. The resulting shade will depend on the amount of oxide used, its quality, and the presence of any other additives.
* *cased* and *overlay* glass comprises two or more layers of coloured glass. An outer vessel is partially inflated (to form a bubble known as a *paraison*), and a gather is then placed inside and blown, so that the layers fuse when they begin to inflate together. Strictly speaking, overlay glass describes any number of layers of coloured glass over a clear body, while cased glass is usually a clear outer layer covering a coloured body, but the terms are often used interchangeably.
* *flashed* glass is made when a vessel is painted with or dipped into another colour, leaving a thin layer on the surface, which could then be cut or engraved. Flashed glass is usually regarded as a less expensive version of cased glass.
* *stained* glass is produced by painting a glass body with a solution of metal oxide. This can produce rich, vibrant colours, and also marbled effects if a number of different oxides are swirled on the surface of a vessel.

DECORATION
"In front of the kiln"
"In front of the kiln" describes hand-made decoration that takes place while the glass is still hot: there are a large number of decorative techniques that involve the manipulation of softened metal.

* *Applied decoration* is the earliest form of decoration on glass. *Trailing* is created by placing thin rods of molten metal on the body of a vessel, and is found on many items of ancient Roman and Egyptian glass. Many wares feature applied blobs of glass, often known as *prunts*. This style is particularly popular in Germany and is found on many drinking glasses, such as the *roemer*. Applied decoration also includes "wings", commonly found on Venetian and *Façon de Venise* pieces, and applied rings, which often feature "milling" (see *below*).

* Other methods of decoration take place "in front of the kiln":
pincering where trailing or other applied decoration is squeezed to give a frilled effect;
combing where trailed, coloured threads are stroked or "combed" to form a wavy design;
milling where vertical grooves similar to those found around the rims of coins are impressed into the glass;
wrythen moulding where softened, vertical ribbing is swirled to encircle the glass creating a spiral effect.

* One of the most important decorative techniqes was developed in Venice in the 15thC. An opaque-white glass was invented which was named *lattimo* ("milk glass").

Used to make beakers, cups and bottles in an attempt to imitate the porcelain wares that were imported from the East, *lattimo* was commonly used to form the basis for many Venetian decorative techniques.

More importantly, *lattimo* was used to create chain-effect decoration on the rims and edges of a wide variety of glassware, such as drinking glasses, *tazzas* and other vessels . It could also be coloured. It is probably best known as lacy inclusions in clear glass called *filigrana* or *latticinio*, but there are many names in Italian for the different styles, such as *vetro a fili* ("thread glass") where the threads ran in parallel lines forming straight or spiral patterns, *vetro a reticello* ("glass with a small network") where the threads crossed to form a lattice, and *vetro a retortoli* ("glass with a twist"), where the threads were twisted together in simple or complex designs.

Other decorative techniques

Almost all other forms of glass decoration are produced by specialist craftsmen, usually in workshops away from the factory, and can be carried out at a much later date than the production of the vessel itself.

There are five main forms.

* Enamelling

Enamel is made from coloured, powdered glass mixed with an oily substance. This is painted onto a glass surface and reheated to fuse the decoration.

* Gilding

Gilt is gold paint, gold dust or gold leaf mixed with a fixative and then fired onto the surface of a glass vessel. Gilt decoration that is not fired is known as "cold gilding" and is less hard-wearing.

A notable variation of gilded decoration is *Zwichengoldglas* (German, "gold between glass"). Popular in Bohemia c.1730–1755, this technique involved the application of gold or silver leaf to the outside of a glass vessel, engraving a design in the leaf, and then placing an outer vessel, or "sleeve", over the top. A disc was used to seal the base.

* Cutting

Cutting is designed to reflect the light and make a glass object even more brilliant. This decorative form was developed principally in England, Ireland and northern Europe in the late 18th and early 19thC. Tools are used to cut into the surface of the glass, leaving sharp-edged patterns in relief. The elaborate designs produced over this period comprised the three main cut patterns: square-ended, "v"-shaped, or hollow.

* Engraving

There are three main methods of engraving glass:
Diamond-point This type of engraving involves the use of a hand tool with a diamond nib that draws lines from which a design can be generated.
Wheel engraving Invented in Germany in the mid-17thC a copper wheel is used to engrave the glass, and before c.1830 was powered only by the foot; after this date water-powered machines were introduced.

An interesting category of engraving is *cameo glass*, where the surface of a glass vessel comprising two or more layers of different-coloured glass is engraved or cut to reveal the colours underneath. The design may stand out in relief if the piece has been cased or overlaid, or may reveal only very thin layers of coloured glass if the vessel has been flashed (see p.11). Invented during Roman times, cameo-cutting techniques have been used to create decorative wares in many glassmaking centres, including Bohemia and Britain in the 19thC.
Stipple engraving This technique involves the use of a diamond needle which is lightly tapped against the surface of the glass creating a pattern of dots. The best stipple engraving comes from the Netherlands.

* Acid etching

This involves covering the surface of a glass vessel with an acid-resistant coating, such as resin, and engraving a design through the coating onto the glass body. The glass is then dipped into acid (most commonly hydrofluoric acid), and the design is traced out by the acid giving a matte or frosted effect.

AUTHENTICITY

When collecting it is important to be aware of the existence of modern reproductions. These can be spotted in a number of ways.

* First,

the texture and appearance of the *metal* should fit the supposed date and location of manufacture. Clear glass made before the 18thC is likely to be discoloured because of the difficulties involved in monitoring the production process. It is useful to have a piece of clear, modern glass to use as a "control" when considering potential purchases.

Under an ultra-violet lamp modern soda glass will emit a green-yellow light; old lead glass will appear blue-purple.

Modern glass tends to be bright in tone, with a thin body.

Older soda glass will not be so bright, small particles may be visible in the glass, and it will feel light in weight.

* *Second*, changes that have taken place in production techniques over the years mean that it is possible to associate some features with particular historical periods.

The most obvious example is the *pontil mark* – the rough part on the base of a piece left by the pontil rod. Items made during the 18thC will have a pontil mark because there was no way to remove it. The development of grinding techniques, especially in England and Ireland in the late 18th to early 19thC, can thus help to date pieces with either polished or ground-out pontil marks.

However the existence or absence of this feature merely acts as a guide and is not a guarantee of authenticity – there are no hard and fast rules – indeed, modern handmade glass is made in almost exactly the same way as items from the 18thC.

The *regularity* of the rim and foot of an item can also be an indication of age: an even shape and thickness may suggest that the piece is relatively modern.

Free-blown glass bodies sometimes appear lop-sided, which can have implications for the age of a piece. Free blowing also leaves fine ripples or *striations* over the surface (visible through a magnifying glass). The surface of mould-blown glass, usually more recent, features no lines.

* *Third*, the proportions of different types of glassware from particular periods have been well documented, and can therefore help to a collector to distinguish between genuine pieces and copies or fakes. For example, Continental, soda-glass copies of 18thC English air twist drinking glasses often look clumsy when compared to the genuine article, with large bowls and heavy feet that make the object appear unbalanced.

* *Fourth*, decoration often enhances the value of a piece, and will sometimes be added to plain items from an earlier period.

The colours of 19thC enamelling tend to be brighter and more solid than earlier examples.

16th and 17thC gilding was usually applied in layers. It is therefore common to find pieces from this period where the gilding has "rubbed off" and only traces are left behind. Later gilding has a flat, more regular appearance.

CARING FOR A COLLECTION
Handling
Handling glass – feeling the texture, the weight and other features of an item – is probably the best way to begin learning about the subject, but always take great care. Some glass should not be over-handled: this includes ancient glass with surfaces that have become oxidized or patinated following a long period of burial, giving an iridescent effect. Also, where pieces have handles, do not use these to lift the item as they are extremely vulnerable, and if damaged will come away from the main body.

Repairs and reconstruction
When buying, damaged pieces should almost always be avoided, although this book attempts to examine areas in which this is not the case.
* Some chips can be successfully removed, usually by grinding, without altering an item's value.
* Missing sections can be replaced, but unless a piece is particularly rare, a replacement part will drastically affect value.
* Look for joins that may indicate a clean break has been repaired.
* Repairs will always require the attention of a professional, and should not be attempted at home: amateur restoration is invariably a disaster.

Cleaning
* Cleaning should be carried out in warm, soapy water using a cloth or soft sponge.
* Dry gently with a soft cloth to avoid damage, but thoroughly to avoid water stains.
* Liquids left in glass vessels over a long period may leave deposits, or cause cloudiness that cannot be removed.
* Where a piece has become cloudy on the inside it is important to have it professionally cleaned (the surface may have to be repolished), but if the item is simply dirty, then household bleach is usually sufficient.
* Do not use bleach on enamelled or gilded glass.
* Do not put antique glass in the dishwasher.

13

GLASSMAKING CENTRES

Princpial glassmaking centres
The main historical glass-producing centres are situated in Europe: the areas pictured above are those most often referred to in this book.

Other centres include, Asia, Scandinavia, Russia (Moscow and St. Petersburg) and the Far East.

Italy
It was the Venetian glass industry that was the first to develop in Europe. Many skilled workers from the Middle East, particularly Damascus in Syria, came to work in Venice in the 15thC, and for the next 300 years Venetian glass was considered to be the best in the world. Altare, near Genoa, was the site of a successful glasshouse, established in the 11thC.

Central Europe
Traditionally, central Europe comprised a large number of small states, many of which were glass producing areas. Bohemia, now in the west of the Czech Republic, was famous for many different styles of glass. Parts of Germany, including Dresden, Potsdam and Nuremberg are all important centres. Hall-in-Tyrol is the site of a famous Austrian glasshouse founded in 1534. Glass was also made in Vienna.

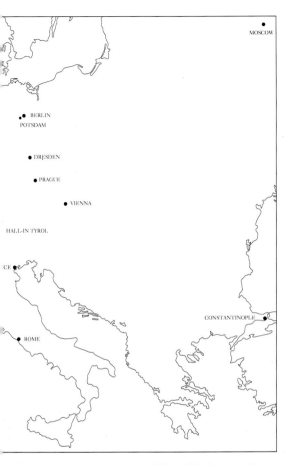

MOSCOW

BERLIN
POTSDAM

DRESDEN

PRAGUE

VIENNA

HALL-IN TYROL

CE

ROME

CONSTANTINOPLE

The Low Countries
Many glassmakers from Venice settled in the Low Countries (Holland, Begium and Luxemburg) in the 16thC, and many factories were established around Antwerp and Liège.

France
The main French factories are situated in Nancy (St. Louis), Baccarat and around Paris (Clichy). Nevers in central France produced some interesting pieces in the 18thC.

Great Britain and Ireland
There are many glassmaking centres in Britain: London, the Midlands (Birmingham and Stourbridge), the west (Bristol), and the north (Newcastle-upon-Tyne). Areas in the south of Ireland such as Waterford and Cork, are famous for cut glass.

Spain
There are two main glass-producing areas in Spain: Catalonia in the north east, and Andalucia in the south around Granada.

The United States
Although not illustrated, the United States has many important glassmaking areas, particularly on the East Coast around New York State and New England.

ANCIENT GLASS

Inlay of a royal head, Egyptian, c.13thC BC

It is most likely that glass was first produced by the accidental presence of sand or quartz in early pottery kilns, although a popular story told by Pliny the Elder (23–79 AD), a Roman naturalist, concerns a merchant who set up camp on a beach and built a fire over a block of soda (a commonly traded commodity at that time), and subsequently found glass under the fire. This must be a fable however, because the heat of a small fire could never be sufficient to create glass which requires a temperature of over 1000°C.

Glass exists naturally in the form of obsidian (a glass-like rock) and pyrites (a crystalline yellow mineral), both resulting from volcanic activity. Manufactured glass seems to have first appeared in Egypt around 1500 BC, but stone beads with a vitreous glaze have also been found from as early as 4000 BC. Dating ancient glass is often a problem, and the earliest pieces that can be accurately dated bear the mark of King Thotmes III (1501–1449 BC). Other items can be dated by their similarity to various artefacts. During this period, the Egyptian army is believed to have returned with some glassmakers following a war with Syria.

Glass became an important Egyptian export, and by 331 BC when Alexander the Great founded the city of Alexandria, the whole of the Middle East was being supplied with Egyptian wares, and some examples even reached as far as England and Northern Europe. Many different forms were produced, including beakers, jugs, vases, flasks, jars and small bottles for oil. Items became more decorative, and highly-coloured mosaic vessels were produced.

The Roman conquest of Egypt led to the next step forward in the development of glassmaking. Previously Rome had been a market for Alexandrian glass, but following the conquest, and the enthusiasm of people such as Cicero who made special mention of Egyptian glass in his writing (54 BC), Egyptian glassmaking techniques were soon adopted and developed by the Romans. The major discovery was glass blowing: before this innovation glass had been coiled around a sand or clay core and then rolled or tooled until it was a complete item. Blowing allowed the glass to be made more finely and evenly, and also made possible the production of larger vessels.

Political stability, established by Caesar Augustus following the defeat of Mark Antony and Cleopatra in 31 BC, allowed the glass industry to expand. Prosperity continued under subsequent leaders, and as well as working to satisfy a healthy market for luxury items, glassmakers made a full range of functional tableware in plain, undecorated glass. Both free and mould-blown items were produced. The Romans also invented many decorative techniques, most notably cameo glass.

As the Roman Empire grew larger, glassmaking skills spread across Europe and the Near East. Glassmakers soon settled in the areas which have since become Germany, France and England, and produced wares for the Empire, but the Middle East with its abundance of raw materials was the principal manufacturer at this time.

The fall of the Roman Empire in the early 5thC BC led to the decline of the glassmaking industry which became regionalized and isolated. All areas retained a basic Roman style but there were no longer the resources and the knowledge to develop further. The Middle East, Spain, Germany and France, as well as northern Italy, had their own glassmaking areas, but for many hundreds of years there were no major changes in forms or techniques.

Ancient Egyptian glass is extremely unusual and difficult to collect. Authenticity can be guaranteed only when buying from a specialist dealer or auction. While large pieces of Roman glass in perfect condition are extremely rare, smaller items are less difficult to obtain. The Romans used small glass bottles or flasks of oil when bathing, and these *unguentarium* were treated as disposable items. These were made in vast quantities between the 1stC BC and the 4thC AD and can be acquired relatively inexpensively. Many were also recycled: glass fragments, known as cullet, were added to the glass mix as a flux and helped to reduce the melting point, thus speeding up the glassmaking process. Evidence of this exists in the form of a wreck discovered in the Eastern Mediterranean, full of pieces of Roman glass.

Many fakes and copies have been produced. These were often not made deliberately to deceive, but have found their way onto the antiquities market, so take care when faced with an apparent bargain.

EGYPTIAN GLASS

A palm column kohl flask with marvered decoration, El-Amarna c.1330 BC; ht 4in (9.9cm); value code A

Identification checklist for Ancient Egyptian glass
1. Does the piece have a bright blue body (other colours are less usual)?
2. Is the body heavy and substantial?
3. Does the decoration look irregular and imperfect?
4. Are there ridges on the surface of the glass?
5. Is it a cylindrical shape?
6. Does the body feature "marvered" and combed decoration (plain examples are rare)?

Early Egyptian glass
Before the founding of the New Kingdom in the Eighteenth Dynasty (c.1540 BC), glass as we know it today had not yet been discovered in Egypt. Vessels were made from faïence, a mixture of quartz sand and an

alkaline substance covered with a vitreous glaze. Glassmaking techniques evolved, and flasks such as the one in the main picture were produced using the "core-forming" method.

The Core-forming technique

A technique for producing "core-formed" vessels was developed in around 1650 BC. A core, often made from a mixture of sand and clay, was moulded into the required shape around a metal rod. Threads of molten glass were wound around the core until the surface was covered. The glass was then rolled or "marvered", on a smooth surface, often a lap stone, decorated on the outer surface with different-coloured spiral threads and marvered again. Rims, handles and bases were added, the rod removed, and finally the core was scraped out.

This core-formed, translucent amber-brown *alabastron* (small bottle) is an unusual colour for Egyptian glass, which was usually bright, opaque blue. Dark green and red examples have also been found (although red is very rare). Other vessels produced using this method include jugs, bowls, *krateriskoi* (vases), and *amphoriskoi* (small containers for oils).

Decoration

The most common form of decoration on Egyptian glass, marvered trails, are usually opaque yellow and white. As techniques developed, decoration became more elaborate with trailing combed into festoons, zig-zags or spiral patterns.

Most Egyptian glass comes from tombs, and among the more interesting of those are the glass inlays used for wooden coffins and tomb furniture. These items are small but form an important and interesting historical record of the times. Glass inlays from coffins found in tombs usually contain hieroglyphics which are often include prayers and dedications to the underworld. The glazed inlay on this wooden panel from the 4thC BC features the words "... may the inhabitants of the necropolis receive you joyously; may your soul go forth to heaven".

Collecting

Egyptian glass is difficult to collect as even small fragments can be quite expensive and hard to date: be sure to buy through specialist dealers or auction rooms. It is not a good idea to buy in the Middle East, as most governments ban the export of antiquities, and any pieces offered to tourists are likely to be fakes.

ROMAN GLASS

A cameo glass flask
c.25 BC–25 AD; ht 3in (7.6cm); value code A

Identification checklist for Roman glass
1. Is the glass blue, amber or clear (others are unusual)?
2. Is the surface iridescent, with an almost metallic shine?
3. Does the piece look flaky and uneven – as if it is extremely old?
4. Is the piece complete?
5. Is the decoration very high quality?
6. Does the piece feel light in weight?
7. If a small bottle, is it in perfect condition?
8. If the piece is more than one colour, does it have a dark (usually blue) body with a white cut design in relief?

Blown glass
Glass blowing was developed in the second half of the 1stC BC in the Syro-Palestinian region. Within 100 years it became the most widely used glass manufacturing technique. It involves placing a gob of molten glass on the end of a blowpipe made from an iron tube, this is then partially inflated into a bubble or "paraison". The craftsman can then blow, shape and decorate the item. The blowpipe is removed and the glass is attached to a pontil or solid rod with a glass seal which is used to finish the neck and rim and to apply handles. Finally the object is placed in an annealing oven, heated and allowed to cool slowly. This reduces the internal strains introduced by continual reheating that can cause the glass to break.

Cameo glass

Cameo is the most characteristic form of Roman glass. It consists of two or more layers, usually a dark base colour covered by opaque white, which was cut to create a relief design. The main picture shows a blown cameo vase, white over cobalt blue, carved with a classical-mythological scene. So few complete pieces exist that although it is heavily encrusted and stained, with a broken rim, it is still very valuable.

* The most famous example of Roman cameo glass is the Portland Vase from the 1stC AD, now in the British Museum. It was brought to England in 1783 and it set a standard that inspired a 19thC revival of the production of cameo glass (see pp.168–169), and led to the development of Josiah Wedgwood's Jasper ware.

Mould-blown glass

The Romans also made items by blowing glass into a wooden, or more rarely, a metal (usually a copper alloy which could be melted down and reused) shaper or mould. Once hardened the piece was removed; any additions – for example, feet and handles, such as the wishbone handle on the head-shaped flask, *above*, were added "in front of the kiln".

Mould blown items appear in a variety of shapes, the most common being square or rectangular. Jugs, vases and bottles in the shape of heads, possibly those of gods, are highly collectable. These were probably used in places of worship such as tombs or in private sanctuaries. There is also a group of pieces moulded as fruits: the body of this flask is a bunch of grapes with a vine leaf on each shoulder.

Collecting

* Some items of Roman glass are surprisingly common. Small bottles and flasks or *unguentarium*, used to hold aromatic oils can be purchased relatively inexpensively. They were regarded by the Romans as disposable items and a huge number were made throughout the Empire. Therefore it is important that they are in near perfect condition.
* Large items will always be more valuable than smaller ones.
* Roman glass is often iridescent due to reactions with various metal oxides during burial.
* The surface should look flaky and not too even.
* Common colours include green-tinted clear glass, blue, green, purple, amber, and rarely white.

A rare group of items are animal-shaped, such as this Eastern Mediterranean mouse flask from the 3rdC AD. They feature moulded or trailed decoration; this style continued to be used in the Middle East and particularly in Spain, where dogs and pigs were made until the 19thC.

21

VENETIAN GLASS

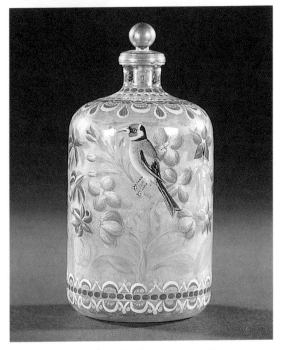

A Venetian enamelled flask and stopper, c.1730

Venice has long been famous for glassmaking, but during Roman times very little glass was made there. The first historical record of Venice as a glassmaking area was in a document from 962, which mentioned a glassworker called "Domenica", and there is also a medieval picture of a glasshouse from around 1040. There is some evidence that there were glassworks in the Venice area making *tesserae* (small glass chips) from the 9–11thC as the fashion for Roman-style mosaics grew in churches in Northern Italy and around the Adriatic coast.

The beginning of the ascendancy of Venice as a trading nation was due to its position as the port of entry nearest to central Europe, and the city's strong navy, necessary to secure safe passage between trading centres. Following the Venetian attack on the cultural centre of Constantinople in 1204, the army returned with plunder that included many glass items, and possibly a number of craftsmen.

The industry began to grow slowly; at the beginning of the 13thC there is mention of a glassmakers' guild, and evidence of Venetian glass being exported across Europe, eventually as far as Great Britain. Indeed, by the 14thC records show that permission was given by Richard II of England

(1367–1400) to a number of Venetian merchants, for the sale of their glassware on the banks of the Thames.

Meanwhile the governors of Venice realized the export potential of their glass, and in 1292 issued a city ordinance making it a capital offence for glassmakers to demonstrate or teach their craft to people from any other nation. The ordinance contained several other strict regulations, and ordered the relocation of the glass industry to the island of Murano, a short distance from the Venetian lagoon, because of the danger of the furnaces to the buildings and residents of the rapidly-expanding city. This had the effect of creating a tightly-knit, secretive, glassmaking community that dominated the population of the island: at the end of the 16thC 3,000 of the 7,000 Muranese were involved with the industry.

Venetian glassmaking received a boost in 1400 when the Mongol conqueror Timur (Tamerlaine) invaded Syria and caused the virtual collapse of the glass industry. Many skilled glassworkers were taken from Damascus to work in Timur's capital, Samarkand in central Asia, while others fled to Venice taking with them their decorative expertise and techniques.

This environment facilitated the development of many new forms and techniques. The invention of *cristallo*, a type of soda glass made with the ashes of barilla (a salt-water marsh plant) that was refined and decoloured using magnesium oxide until almost transparent, was a major leap forward. In common use by the end of the 15thC, *cristallo* was well-adapted to blowing and could be drawn into fine and fantastic shapes, giving a light and fragile appearance.

Venetian glassmakers reintroduced and improved Roman decorative techniques, such as arrangements of coloured glass canes known as *millefiori* ("a thousand flowers"). During experiments with coloured glass in the 15thC, craftsmen discovered a milk-white glass which they called *lattimo*. Pieces are rarely found as plain *lattimo* wares, but the technique was the basis of many other decorative forms. It was used to create chain-effect decoration on the rims and edges of a wide variety of glassware, and could also be coloured. It is probably best known as lacy inclusions in clear glass called *latticino* or *latticinio*, but there are many names in Italian for the different styles, such as *vetro a fili* ("thread glass"), *vetro a reticello* ("glass with a small network"), *vetro a retortoli* ("glass with a twist"), and *vetro di trino* ("glass of lace"). Syrian influences were seen in gilding and enamelling on translucent, coloured glass.

Venice became relatively less important as a glassmaking centre for a number of reasons. The discovery of the Cape route to the Indies in 1488 affected the prominence of the city as a gateway to the East. In spite of the restrictions some workers did leave Murano and took their expertise with them to other European centres. Experimentation abroad led to developments that eclipsed the use of *cristallo* as a metal for high quality wares, most notably the invention of lead crystal in Britain at the end of the 17thC.

VENETIAN TAZZAS

*A Venetian enamelled low tazza with a painted centre
c.1500; ht 10½ in (27cm); value code B*

Identification checklist for Venetian *tazzas*
1. Does the *tazza* have a wide, flat top?
2. Does it have a low, spreading foot (others are more unusual)?
3. Are the rim and foot folded?
4. Does the piece have a plate-style lip or an upturned rim (flat examples are exceptional)?
5. Is there a large amount of applied decoration, probably gilding and/or enamelling?
6. Is the decoration in good condition?
7. Does the *tazza* feel surprisingly light?

Venetian *tazzas*
Following the Mongol invasion of Syria by Tamerlaine in 1402 and the deportation of its glass craftsmen, Venice quickly replaced the East as the world's centre of fine glassmaking. Many decorative techniques from Syria and other parts of the Middle East were adopted by the Venetians, and can be seen in the *tazza* in the main picture, which has an enamelled centre painted in ochre, green and blue, and a border decorated with gilt scales.

Features
The name *tazza* comes from the Italian for "cup", but rather than cups as we understand them, these were very shallow, sometimes flat dishes, derived from the silver drinking vessels used in

Rome. They always have a foot of some sort, the most common being low and spreading, but occasionally they have high, elegant, typical wine glass stems.

Tazzas were made with either a small, upturned rim such as the one on the main picture, or a plate-style lip as on this beautiful

24

gilded and enamelled example.
* Flat *tazzas* are exceptionally
rare and should be treated with
suspicion: rims and feet are sometimes removed while smoothing
out chips.

Function
Tazzas were a luxury item, owned
primarily by the wealthy (many
feature the crests of important
families) and were highly valued.
They were often given as wedding presents. The fact that so
many are in good condition indicates that they were used for
decoration and special occasions,
not for everyday use.

Venetian *tazzas* appear in many
16thC paintings throughout
Europe which give clues as to
how they were used: some as
small trays for items such as
glasses, others as dishes for fruit
or sweetmeats, and in a detail of
Bacchus by Caravaggio
(1571–1610) a *tazza* is shown
filled with red wine. This is a
large bowl-shaped *tazza* (11¾ in,
30cm in diameter) c.1500, with a
spreading, ribbed foot to aid stability. Less ornate than other
Venetian *tazzas*, this example has
only a coloured foot and rim.

Decoration
No other type of glass item during this period gave the craftsmen
such a large area on which to
demonstrate their decorative
skills. Styles of decoration
include: ribbing, enamelling,
tooling, gilding and trailing.
* Gilding and enamelled decoration were usually applied to the
top surface, making it very
vulnerable to wear.

Condition
While slight wear to the foot of a
tazza may not significantly affect
its value – the *tazza* in the main
picture has a slight crack on the
foot – any damage to the decoration may reduce its value by more
than a third.

Towards the end of the 17thC
the Venetians began to introduce
new methods of glass decoration
and *tazzas* became more flamboyant. This is a *latticinio* or *filigrana
tazza* with a wide, shallow bowl
set on a knopped baluster stem.
Filigrana was created by laying
out canes of milk-white glass
called *lattimo* (see p.29) in patterns on a flat surface, and combining them with a bubble of
blown cristallo. Usually included
in a clear glass body, stripes of
colours such as red and blue are
sometimes found within the
designs. The technique developed on the island of Murano to
which Venetian glass makers
were banished in the 13thC,
because of the risk of fire to the
city. Items made from *filigrana*
were fashionable for nearly 200
years and were widely imitated.

This small, cup-shaped *tazza*
from around 1700, also made with
latticinio decoration, has a rudimentary (very small) foot. This
tazza was used as a drinking vessel and was designed to be held
until all the contents had been
consumed – it is unstable when
set down on a flat surface.
* *Latticinio* decoration is also
found in combination with bands
of coloured glass.

Copies
* Some copies of *tazzas* were
made in the late 19thC but these
are very clear and heavy; they
were not really made to deceive,
but as an appreciation of earlier
techniques.

FAÇON DE VENISE

*A Façon de Venise tazza from Antwerp or South Netherlands
c.16thC; dia. 7⅔ in (19.5cm); value code B*

Identification checklist for *Façon de Venise* serpent-stemmed glasses
1. Is the metal greyer and more bubbly than Venetian *cristallo*?
2. Does the piece feel relatively light in weight?
3. If the goblet has a stem with applied "wings", do they resemble serpents?
4. Are the wings symmetrical and elaborate?
5. If the stem decoration is coloured is it blue (perhaps with red, white and ochre detail)?

Façon de Venise
Façon de Venise means "in the Venetian style", and is a term used to describe high quality glassware with Venetian influence, which was made throughout Europe in the 16th and 17thC. The *tazza* in the main picture is a classic shape, it has a grey tint and the bubbly effect produced by soda glass, and will thus feel light in weight. A typical example, it is largely plain, with traces of gilding on the rim, three milled bands on the underside, and a wrythen-moulded knop.

Filigrana
The goblet, *right*, c.1650, is made of filigree, a type of glass first produced in Murano. Filigree (from the Italian *filigrana* meaning "thread grained"), describes threads of glass (usually opaque

white) that are embedded in clear glass to form a fine network. Here twisted vertical threads alternate with pale blue ribbons: the quality shows how the production of *Façon de Venise* progressed far beyond simple reproduction.

The Low Countries

In spite of the penalty of death for the disclosure of industrial secrets, many Venetian wokers moved west during the 16thC to satisfy the demand for luxury glass. Some settled in the Low Countries, and factories were established which reproduced glass items using Venetian blowing skills and decorative techniques.

* One sure way to distinguish between the two will be if a piece features diamond-point engraving: this never appeared on Venetian glass.

Identification

Some *Façon de Venise* pieces are very difficult to tell apart from those actually made in Venice. The *latticinio* covered goblet, *right*, has defied attribution, and is classified simply as "Venice/Low Countries". *Façon de Venise* items tend to have less decoration than their Italian counterparts, on clear pieces the metal may be slightly greyer, and there may be more bubbles. In fact, age and quality are more important determinants of value than geographical origin.

Britain

Venetian techniques were first introduced in c.1549. The Frenchman Jean Carré, and later the Venetian Giacomo Verzelini, led the industry in Britain.

Serpent-stemmed glasses

These serpent-stemmed goblets have a Venetian shape but the vast majority were Dutch-made. They are unusual but beautifully-made items, with complicated stems featuring coloured and tooled decoration. This is invariably blue, as on these examples, and will sometimes include white, red and ochre detail.

* A word of warning: check the "wings" as it is not unusual to find a glass that has been damaged on one side, with a corresponding piece removed from the other side. These sorts of repairs can be difficult to spot.

* The more elaborate the wings, the more valuable a serpent-stemmed glass will be.

* The German *Historismus* movement (see pp.42–43) made many, very good copies of these glasses at the end of the 19thC, which are remarkably difficult to distinguish from the originals. Some regularly appear in auction with an earlier date, and whilst both types are expensive, a 19thC goblet will fetch only a third as much as one from the 16thC.

* Beware: the market for these goblets tends to be quite volatile.

OTHER VENETIAN GLASS

A Venetian enamelled armorial goblet c.1500; ht 5¼ in (13.2cm); value code A

Identification checklist for enamelled Venetian glass from the 16th–18thC

1. Does the piece feel relatively light in weight?
2. Is the glass slightly cloudy?
3. Is the decoration hand painted in a spontaneous style (look for irregularities from brush strokes)?
4. Does the piece have a narrow, folded rim?
5. Does the piece have a slightly irregular appearance, suggesting that it was made by hand?
6. If there is a crest, can it be identified?

Other Venetian glass

Venetian glassmakers experimented with many different forms and techniques. Renaissance Venetian styles have influenced craftsmen in many centres down to the present day.

The goblet in the main picture was one of six ordered for the town of Bardejou in Bohemia in 1500. The characteristic Venetian shape continues to be imitated and many copies are difficult to distinguish from the original.

These goblets, however, were documented and can be positively attributed. The tooled decoration and hand-painted crest are also typical; the slight uneveness of the painting around the rim, and the lop-sided join between the bowl and the base, indicate the age of the piece.

Decorated wares

Although painting and enamelling on glass were not exclusive to Venice, the style and quality were of the highest standard, and the painting was characteristically free and naturalistic. A wide variety of wares were produced.

This tankard illustrates the flamboyant nature of Venetian decoration, with typically vibrant colours and a highly ornate handle. The mould-blown base and tooled foot are more unusual in Venetian glass made after 1700, as is the *latticinio* decoration such as the band around the middle. The cloudiness in the glass may be due either to crizzling or to water staining (it is now possible to polish away water staining). The flower decoration which includes roses, lilies and hyacinths suggests that the tankard was made for export to the Ottoman Empire.
* The East became a more important market during the 18thC as glass centres in Britain, the Low Countries and Bohemia became more productive.
* Make sure that the enamelling has been applied by hand: look for slight irregularities and visible brush strokes. Later pieces were transfer printed.
* Some items were decorated

with crests and other armorial designs: check that these are attributable as on later copies the crests are usually fictitious.

Lattimo
One of the most important decorative techniqes was developed in the 15thC, when an opaque-white glass called *lattimo* ("milk glass") was invented.

Lattimo was used to make beakers, cups and bottles, such as the one *above*, in an attempt to imitate porcelain wares imported from the East. This bottle from the mid-18thC is unusually large, and was probably used as a serving bottle or decanter. The lack of decoration adds to its rarity, as does the date of manufacture – *lattimo* wares were not often made at this time.
* Many Venetian decorative techniques were based on *lattimo*.

Undecorated wares
Undecorated Venetian glass is difficult to identify, while decorative styles such as engraving, enamelling and tooling are highly distinctive. However, relative lightness, folded rims, cloudy

metal, and small bubbles and imperfections, such as those seen *below*, can aid identification. This bowl and plate made in the mid-17thC have been crudely rib moulded, and have a high kick in the base, another typical feature.

Imitators and forgers have failed to reproduce all these characteristics successfully.
* Some Venetian glassworkers moved to Britain and exerted a considerable influence on 16th and 17thC British glass.

29

CENTRAL EUROPEAN GLASS

A Viennese transparent-enamelled goblet by Gottlob Mohn, signed and dated 1816

Central Europe (an area that now comprises Germany, Austria, Hungary, Poland and Czechoslovakia), imported all glass supplies from Rome in the 2nd and 3rdC. By the 12thC however, a domestic industry had been established based on *waldglas* or "forest glass", a pale green, transparent metal made using ash from ferns and bracken found in forests throughout the area. Distinctive German vessels began to develop, including the *roemer* (a drinking vessel with an ovoid bowl and a hollow stem), the *kuttrolf* (a decanter with a large surface area for cooling spirits), and the *nuppenbecher* (a prunted beaker). A Venetian influence is visible in the style of decoration: most often "prunts" or applied blobs of glass, or trailed decoration.

The next major period of innovation in in glassmaking in central Europe began during the Renaissance, when art, literature and politics across the Continent were influenced by Ancient Greek and Roman forms and ideas. The movement developed in northern Italy in the late 14thC, reached England and northern areas of Europe by the late 15thC, and led to the development of new styles and techniques.

Glass produced in the Low Countries (including Holland,

Belgium and Luxembourg) during the Middle Ages, was principally *waldglas* made in traditional German forms. In the 16thC, however, Italian glassworkers, including Giacomo Verzelini (d.1606) settled in Holland and Belgium, and glasshouses began to produce some fine examples of *Façon de Venise* glassware (see pp.26–27).

Façon de Venise was also produced at many centres in Germany, including Dresden, Munich and Nuremberg, but medieval German vessels were also made for local markets. German craftsmen became expert at several methods of decoration, including many types of enamelling. One particularly notable innovation was *Schwarzlot*, which involved painting thinly-applied, transparent enamels (usually black, but iron red is also found) onto a clear glass body. Sometimes gilt highlighting was also added.

Engraving was popular in both central Europe and the Low Countries between the 16th and 18thC. Diamond-point engraving began in Europe c.1560, and wheel engraving was first carried out in Germany, particularly around Bohemia. These techniques spread to the Low Countries where craftsmen produced extremely high quality work. The further development of wheel engraving was given a boost by the invention of a heavier, more substantial and better quality metal in around 1700 made from potash (potassium carbonate) mixed with chalk or lime (calcium carbonate), and by the introduction of water-powered cutting wheels. This led to the production of glass cut in high relief, in a rock-crystal style. A large number of goblets and beakers were also engraved in other centres in central Europe.

"Gold sandwich glass" or *Zwichengoldglas*, is another notable German decorative form, and the most famous exponent of this skill was probably Johann Mildner (1763–1808). At the end of the 18th and beginning of the 19thC, Bohemia became a centre for experimentation with different types of coloured glass. This group includes: Friedrich Egermann's ruby and gold topaz chloride stains, and *Lithyalin*, a coloured, marbled glass made to imitate agate and other semiprecious stones; Josef Reidel's yellow/green uranium glass known as *Annagelb* and *Annagrün*; and Count von Buquoy's opaque black *Hyalith* (see pp.40–41 and pp.46–47).

19thC German and Bohemian glass was characterized by two main fashions. The first was the Biedermeier style, based around an ideal of "comfortable simplicity", and popularized by the expanding middle classes in Germany. Typical forms and techniques from the Biedermeier period, c.1825–1840, include straight-sided beakers decorated with translucent coloured enamels, and new styles of coloured glass, such as those mentioned earlier. The second 19thC fashion, c.1870, was *Historismus*, a revival of antique German forms with brightly-coloured decoration.

In the 19thC, glasshouses in Holland and Belgium such as Val St. Lambert and Vonêche produced extremely high quality wares in a European style. Unfortunately individual pieces are not easy to attribute to particular factories.

DIAMOND ENGRAVED GLASS

A Dutch green-tinted, diamond engraved serving bottle dated 1676; ht 9⅜ in (24cm); value code A

Identification checklist for 17th and 18thC diamond engraved glass
1. Is the engraving shallow and highly skilled?
2. Are the engraved lines ragged and slightly broken?
3. Does the decoration feature a Dutch inscription, or a Dutch subject (British subjects are less common)?
4. If signed, is the signature on the foot (signatures found anywhere else are more unusual)?
5. If stipple engraved, is the subject allegorical, Jacobin, or a portrait?
6. Can the design be seen clearly only at a certain angle?

Diamond-point engraving
An ancient method of glass decoration, diamond engraving became particularly popular in the Low Countries, c.1600–1800. It involves using a diamond or metal-tipped stylus to scratch a pattern on the surface of the glass. The cutting is not deep and lines are often slightly ragged and broken, in contrast to the hard lines created by wheel engraving.

The serving bottle in the main picture was engraved by Willem van Heemskerk (1613–1692), a cloth merchant, poet and playwright from Leiden, for whom glass decoration was a hobby. His work, often found on bottles and *roemers*, is unusual because it features calligraphic designs and detailed inscriptions: only very few craftsmen used calligraphy in their engraving.

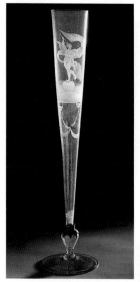

subsequently copied in Holland, is often diamond-point engraved, such as the example, *below left*, showing the arms of William of Orange. The tall, delicately-knopped stem and elegant proportions are characteristic of this type of drinking glass.
* These glasses were engraved exclusively for the Dutch market, and are mainly armorial.

Stipple-point engraving
In spite of changing fashions abroad, diamond point engraving remained popular in the Netherlands. It was gradually refined, and c.1780 a technique known as stipple engraving was introduced. Instead of using the diamond stylus to cut lines, it was tapped on the surface to create designs consisting of minute dots. The density of the dots created the effect of light and shade.

From the mid-17thC a number of tall flute glasses were made in the *Façon de Venise* style, most now belong to museum collections although some are offered for sale. They were usually made as commemorative pieces or to special commission. This glass is signed on the bowl *fc M*, an abbreviation for *fecit* (made by) "M" and is dated 1662. Items were more commonly signed and dated on the pontil, as on the bottle in the main picture.

Another group of diamond point engraved glasses are Newcastle Light Balusters (see pp.84–85). This English form, which was

The detail on stipple-engraved glass is often so fine that the design can only be seen clearly when held up to the light at the same angle as the stylus struck the glass. The most famous craftsmen were Frans Greenwood (1680–1761), and David Wolff (1732–1798), who engraved this glass with a portrait of William V of Holland, c.1780.
* Designs include allegorical subjects, portraits, and Jacobin motifs supporting the French Revolution.

Collecting
* On early pieces, minor damage will not significantly affect value.
* A signed piece is worth twice as much as one that is unsigned. Stipple-engraved pieces are more often signed and are valuable.

BELGIAN GLASS

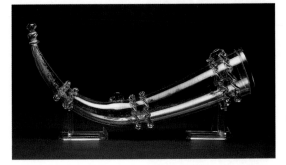

A medieval-style glass drinking horn, Antwerp c.1580; lgth 11½ in (30cm); value code B

Identification checklist for Liège lattice glassware from the 18thC
1. Is part of the structure made from open lattice of glass rods?
2. Is the piece free from cut and engraved decoration?
3. Are the rims, edges and solid structural parts embellished with tooled decoration?
4. Does the decoration appear spontaneous, as if it was carried out "in front of the kiln"?
5. Is the glass colourless (coloured pieces are very unusual)?
6. Does it contain bubbles and appear slightly grey in tone?
7. Does the piece feel relatively light in weight?

Belgian glass
With some exceptions, it is difficult to identify the exact origin of glassware made in what are now the modern countries of Belgium and Holland, during the 16–18thC. The multitude of *Façon de Venise* wares is one example, and such pieces are usually attributed to the "Low Countries". However, two particular areas in modern Belgium have been major glassmaking areas for hundreds of years.

Antwerp
The Flemish capital Antwerp, has a history of glassmaking going back to Roman times, and whilst glass from the Low Countries was heavily influenced by Venetian design, glass from Antwerp in particular, has a more Germanic style. The drinking horn in the main picture, made around 1580, has a medieval feel typical of

Antwerp glass. Generally the only decoration found is trailed and tooled; some pieces were engraved, but in general the glass tended to be too thin and brittle for this style of decoration.

Liège
The other main area for glass production is situated in the south, around the cities of Liège and Namur. Liège was well placed geographically to import *barilla*, a form of soda derived from a Spanish plant which produced clear soda glass. Again many items of unattributable origin were made including some very good cut glass in the British style. Liège did produce one or two unique pieces, particularly intricate woven glass baskets, vases and other wares. It is also thought that many Newcastle Light Balusters (see pp.84–85) were made in Liège.

The holy water stoop *below*, illustrates the complicated nature of the weaving, it is extremely delicate and should be handled with great care. Woven glass such as this was made over a long period from the mid-18thC to the early 20thC, earlier pieces tend to be lighter, less clear and generally better made. All the decoration was carried out while the glass was still hot "in front of the kiln", and is never cut or engraved. The function of these items appears to be purely decorative, but it is also possible that they were made to demonstrate the skill of the glassmaker. Other wares included mould-blown vessels with moulding, fluting and spiral ribbing.

These drinking glasses are comparable in quality to late 18thC English lead crystal and are equally heavy, but they are often larger in size, slightly greyer in tone, and always feature either engraved or cut decoration.

Val St. Lambert (est. 1826)
Also in the Liège/Namur area are the Cristalleries du Val St Lambert (VSL). Pieces by VSL were always of the highest standard, but its styles were so heavily influenced by the rest of Europe that they are difficult to distinguish from similar items produced in other countries.

* Parts of the structure sometimes became over-thin or were broken during production, damage of this sort is acceptable.
* Another group of wares usually attributed to Liège, are large "toys" or novelty items – for example, swords and trumpets. These can be confused with Nailsea glass, but are usually more accurately made and more colourful than their British counterparts.

Vonêche (1779–1830)
In 1779 the Empress Marie-Therese granted a licence to P. N. Mathy to produce glass at a small village in the Ardennes called Vonêche; the factory operated until 1830 producing high quality crystal wares. It also supplied blanks to many famous cutting workshops around Europe.

A few of their designs are more easily identifiable, following the establishment of an individual design movement which flourished from around 1880–1939. These bronze-mounted overlay vases with acid-cut cameo motifs are one style developed by VSL, and were inspired by oriental pieces made in ivory.

35

SCHWARZLOT

A Nuremberg Schwarzlot beaker
c.1675; ht 5in (13cm); value code A

Identification checklist for *Schwarzlot* glass

1. Is the design black, brown and/or red?
2. Is it highly detailed and beautifully executed?
3. Is the glass item itself small and unremarkable?
4. If the piece is a tumbler, does it have three ball feet?
5. If there is a signature, does it belong to an artist rather than a factory?
6. Is the piece gilded?
7. Does the clear body have a soft tone?
8. Is the design painted and not printed onto the glass?

Johann Schaper (1621–1670)

Around the mid-17thC a new decorative technique was developed in Nuremberg by Johann Schaper. He was a *hausmaler*, a freelance painter who had previously specialized in the decoration of stained glass windows. His method involved freehand painting in either an iron-red (*eiserot*) or black (*schwarzlot*) enamel wash. When the painting was finished, it was annealed to fix it to the surface. This glass is now known as *Schwarzlot*, and remained popular until the mid-18thC. Schaper practised his skills on a number surfaces other than glass, including porcelain.

Early *Schwarzlot* glass

Most early examples can be attributed to Schaper or his followers: the most important of these were Johann Faber and Abraham Helmack. They decorated low cylindrical beakers, usually with three flattened ball, or bun feet, such as the one in the main picture. This glass is painted with a continuous landscape scene. Signed "MF", this anonymous craftsman is likely to have been part of Schaper's circle.
* The glass items on which the artists worked were often incidental to the design itself, and were used simply because of their availability.

Subjects

The most common subjects found on early *Schwarzlot* glass include hunting scenes, tales from mythology, Romantic landscapes, coats of arms, harbour scenes, and humorous dwarves.

Ignaz Preissler (b.1670)

Together with his father Daniel (1636–1733), Ignaz Preissler developed the production of *Schwarzlot* glass. He worked in both *Eiserot* and *Schwarzlot*, and also used gilt which added depth and richness to his designs.

Flasks are very unusual, and this signed example from around 1725 is exceptionally rare because it shows an extended view of old Vienna, with the goddess Europa on the reverse.
* Other Preissler designs include garlands of leaves, branches and flowers, with interwoven figures, Chinoiserie motifs, and some heraldic emblems. Preissler also worked on porcelain.

Other craftsmen of the time attempted to emulate Preissler's technique, but were unsuccessful. A revival of *Schwarzlot* glass took place towards the end of the 19thC, spurred on by the *Historismus* movement (see pp.42–43). Louis Lobmeyr, a Viennese industrialist and glass designer was the driving force behind the renewal of production. His factory made very good quality copies, painted with hunting or German folk and peasant scenes. Other factories tried to produce *Schwarzlot*, but without the same success.
* These glasses are difficult to distinguish from the originals, but luckily most Lobmeyr pieces are signed with the factory monogram.
* Glass on later versions has a very bright tone.

Beware

* Some later copies were transfer printed rather than painted. This should be obvious when the design is viewed through a magnifying glass.
* Damage to the enamelled decoration may reduce the value by up to three-quarters.

This *Schwarzlot* armorial bowl from around 1736 is unsigned but can be attributed to Preissler or another good maker. It features a motto, *per ardua bonum*, and the arms of the Cruikshank family, originally from Aberdeenshire, who subsequently became wealthy merchants in Amsterdam. It is probably a marriage piece.

ZWISCHENGOLDGLAS

A lower Austrian Zwischengoldglas armorial tumbler dated 1794; ht 4½ in (12cm); value code C

Identification checklist for *Zwischengoldglas*
1. Is the decoration between two layers of glass?
2. Does it contain gold and/or silver?
3. Is the glass body clear (coloured grounds are less common)?
4. Is the piece a cylindrical beaker (other forms are rare)?
5. Is there a medallion in the walls or the base of the glass?
6. Is the outer surface faceted?
7. Is the subject of the design religious, romantic, armorial, or a landscape or hunting scene?
8. If there is a portrait, is the piece signed and dated?

Zwischengoldglas
In around 1725 Bohemian glassmakers developed a decorative technique based on Roman *Fondi d'ors*, and known as *Zwischengoldglas* meaning "double gilded glass". It was created by sandwiching gold leaf between two layers of glass. The style was very popular between 1730 and 1750, enjoyed a revival at the end of the 18thC, and again at the end of the 19thC. The most

frequently-found items are cylindrical beakers, such as the one in the main picture, because the form was well suited to the technique.

Technique
Zwischengoldglas is produced by applying gold leaf to the outside of a glass vessel, engraving the surface using a diamond stylus, and then protecting the decoration by sliding a second vessel or

"sleeve" over the first. The glass on the inside had a lip about ⅜ in (1cm) from the top, and the second vessel fitted tightly under this. The glass sleeve was bottomless, and a disc was cut to fit the base; the air space in between was sealed with laquer resin.

* The gold leaf was sometimes highlighted with red, green and occasionally white enamels.
* Silver foil decoration was also used, but was less popular because it had a tendency to oxidize and turn black, even after it was sealed.

Blue-tinted examples of *Zwischengoldglas* are very rare: this beaker is worth up to a third more than others with more usual red and gold decoration. Due to the denseness of the colour, the basal medallion has been inserted so it can only be seen from underneath instead of from above.

This beaker from around 1730 is an early example of *Zwischengoldglas*. It is a more unusual piece with polychrome laquering on silver foil, cut with vertical facets. The religious figure is typical; other popular designs include hunting and garden scenes, and armorial designs.

Johann Mildner (1763–1808)
The best *Zwischengoldglas* was produced during the first revival period towards the end of the 18thC, by Johann Joseph Mildner. He worked almost exclusively on tankards and beakers, which were usually straight sided. He specialized in medallions or miniature portraits, usually gilt or silver motifs on red lacquer grounds, which were inserted into the walls and bases of the items. Pieces are often signed and dated, on either the base or the reverse of the painted subject. The beaker in the main picture is signed *1794 Mildner fec.* Usually light cutting was applied to "finish" the item on the base or the rim.

The silver and gold design on this beaker has been highlighted in the more common colours of red, green and brown; white was used very rarely. It features a characteristic romantic design.

Late 19thC *Zwischengoldglas*
* Some *Zwischengoldglas* was made during the 19thC, but towards the end of the century, copies were made in Venice. They are good copies, but the metal is of inferior quality and the decoration is coarse.
* The Austrian firm Moser (and later the Belgian firm Val St. Lambert) produced a number of tumblers with discs in the base, usually decorated with wild flowers. These have factory marks, and are heavier and more tapering than the originals.

Collecting
* It is important to check that the seal is in place – if it is missing the decoration will deteriorate.
* Check for cracks in both layers of glass which can be hard to find.
* Where medallions are painted, the quality of the picture or design is an important determinant of value.

BIEDERMEIER

A Viennese transparent-enamelled beaker by Gottlob Mohn dated 1812; ht 3¾ in (9.5cm); value code A

Identification checklist for Biedermeier-style glassware
1. Is the piece a straight-sided or waisted beaker?
2. Is the painted decoration very high quality?
3. Does the design feature a Germanic subject or motif?
4. Is there any gilt detailing?
5. Is the decoration in good condition?
6. If signed, does the signature appear on the base or the reverse of the painting?
7. If the piece is *Lithyalin*, is it cut?

Biedermeier glass
The Biedermeier style characterized a period of middle class prosperity in Germany following the end of the Napoleonic Wars (c.1815–1845). Derived from blond wood furniture with black detail that was produced in North Germany and Scandinavia, it was adopted by many manufacturers of decorative arts.

Samuel and Gottlob Mohn
The masters of the medium were Samuel Mohn (1762–1815) and his son Gottlob (1789–1825). They worked in thinly applied,

translucent enamels most commonly on straight-sided beakers. Subjects included panoramic views, and romantic and allegorical designs. Gottlob moved to Vienna in 1811 and influenced a number of craftsmen. The beaker in the main picture, decorated with a lawyer accepting a bribe, is signed *G.Mohn f.a. Wien*, and dated 1812.

Anton Kothgasser (1759–1851)
One of the most prolific enamellers to be influenced by the Mohns was Anton Kothgasser.

Originally a painter at the Royal Vienna Porcelain Manufactory, he was introduced to the technique of glass painting by Gottlob Mohn.
* His designs included views of landscapes and towns (especially of Vienna), portraits of personalities, allegorical representations and animal or plant motifs.
* Kothgasser's pieces were sometimes signed, often on the base rim, with either his initials "A.K." or his name in full.

This typical red, hexagonal *Lithyalin* beaker attributed to Egermann, has been brushed with metal oxides and lustres to simulate veining and marbling.

After 1814, another glass form was produced, especially popular with Kothgasser, known as the *Ranftbecher* – a waisted trumpet-shaped vessel on a cogwheel base. This glass, probably a love token, is decorated unusually with tarot cards, and a French motto is inscribed on the reverse ("Leur union est notre force").
* Viennese Biedermeier glasses were made as expensive souvenirs, and were given as gifts.
* Other famous enamellers of the time included C. von Scheidt, Andreas Mattoni (Karlsbad), and C.F. Hoffmeister (Vienna).

This spa beaker from Egermann's workshop in Bottendorf has a more unusual dark green background; occasionally blue and purple *Lithyalin* is also found. Pieces are often cut, sometimes with gilt detailing on rims and feet.

Friedrich Egermann (1777–1864)

A glass blower and decorator, and amateur chemist from northern Bohemia, Egermann is best known for his invention of *Lithyalin*, a highly polished opaque glass that was sometimes decorated with swirling colours to imitate agate and other semi-precious stones. The technique was patented in 1829.
* A similar technique was developed by Count von Buquoy who produced a black agate-like glass in 1817, and a similar dark red glass called *Hyalith* in 1819.

Collecting

* Signatures add to value, and if present, are usually found on the base or reverse of the painting.
* As they were not designed for use, the condition of enamelled or *Lithyalin* wares is important.
* Watch out for restoration on *Lithyalin* and *Hyalith* as ceramic methods are sometimes used, and repairs can be difficult to spot.

Other 19thC German glass

Other decorative styles of the period involved the use of colour, such as uranium and overlay glass (see pp.46–47).

HISTORISMUS

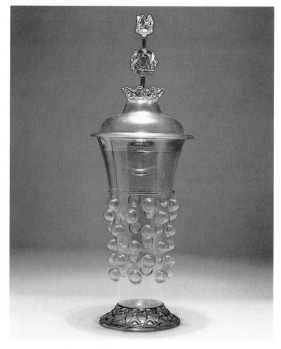

A large green-tinted "Titian Humpen" and cover by Köln-Ehrenfeld c.1886; 15¾in (40 cm); value code C

Identification checklist for *Historismus* wares
1. Does the piece feel heavy?
2. Is the glass free from imperfections?
3. Is the body colour a shade of green or amber?
4. Is the piece based on an antique German vessel?
5. Does it have an exaggerated form?
6. Is the piece over-decorated?
7. If enamelled, is the decoration good quality and highly coloured?
8. If armorial, is the crest ficticious or does it belong to a large town (family crests are unusual)?

The *Historismus* movement
Following the re-establishment of the German Empire in 1871, many styles of antique German glass and other traditional forms within the decorative arts, were reproduced as part of an effort to establish a unified national heritage. This movement was part of a *Historismus* trend in Europe where old Venetian styles were also being copied. Many German pieces were based on medieval and Renaissance glass of the Tyrol and Bohemia as well as the area around the German-Polish border. Popular forms included *Humpen* (a tall cylindrical beer glass), *Roemer* (15th and 16thC drinking vessel), *Kuttrolf* (a cooling bottle) and *Daumenglas* (a barrel-shaped beaker).

Köln-Ehrenfeld

One manufacturer of high quality *Historismus* wares was Köln-Ehrenfeld situated on the Rhine. The crystal *"Titian Humpen"* in the main picture is typical of the "Old German" items produced at this glassworks. It has a medieval *humpen* shape, but the ornate, caged foot and finial would not have existed on an old piece.

* *Historismus* copies of antique German vessels are characterized by their exaggerated decoration.

Vessels were also produced for a wider market, with good quality, highly coloured, enamelled decoration, often including crests and other armorial motifs. The examples *above*, show the exaggerated forms and over-decoration common to *Historismus* pieces.

* The body colour is usually green or amber in varying shades.
* In this group, wares from premier manufacturers are collectable, but others have little value.
* Some pieces are very large, up to 39in (1m) high, but common to all *Historismus* items, quality is the major determinant of value.

Identification

* Pieces are occasionally signed: the signature will be engraved if the item is blown, and engraved or enamelled if it is enamelled. It is usually the highest quality vessels that are signed.
* Some high quality wares are difficult to distinguish from original antique German wares: often only the signature can determine the date of manufacture.
* The most accurate way to date an item is to refer to the contemporary catalogues of the 19thC factories. If the piece does not appear, then check the glass body: the glass used to make *Historismus* wares will be heavy and free from imperfections due to improved production techniques. On larger items there will be no "wipe" marks where the glass has run while wet.

* On *Historismus* wares, the coats of arms that appear are usually those of large towns or are fictitious, although a small number feature family crests.

The Austrian firm Lobmeyr was another important manufacturer of *Historismus* pieces. This decanter, c.1880, has a typical antique shape. It is signed and engraved in the Baroque style.

19THC GERMAN ENGRAVED GLASS

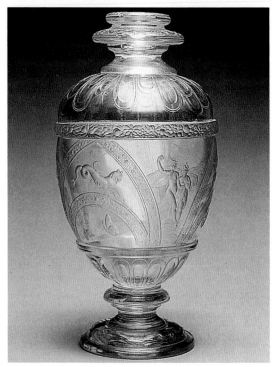

Engraved "rock crystal" vase, possibly Lobmeyr c.1870; ht 10in (25cm); value code C

Identification checklist for 19thC German engraved glass
1. Is the engraving fluid and sophisticated?
2. Does it feature a Germanic motif – for example a landscape or woodland scene?
3. Is the design detailed and well drawn?
4. If coloured, does the piece feel relatively heavy?
5. Is the cutting and engraving heavy and ornate?
6. Is the piece signed by the artist?
7. Is the signature hidden within the engraved design?

19thC Bohemian engraving
Bohemian engraved glass underwent a change of style during the 19thC. The stiff and formal designs which characterized the the late 18thC and the Napoleonic Wars, became more fluid and sophisticated.

Engravers in Bohemia were without equal; the covered vase in the main picture, deeply "carved" to imitate rock crystal with classical-mythological figures, is a fine example of their skills.
* Rock crystal-style wares usually have large bodies.

Subjects
In the 19thC craftsmen began to
work with coloured glass, and
vessels with more interesting
shapes. This gave them greater
scope for their designs and popular subjects included idealized
landscapes, woodland scenes,
hunting, horses and battles.
* Pieces engraved with grape-
vines are relatively inexpensive –
a good way to start a collection.

The most characteristic form of
Bohemian engraving was on overlay or flashed glass bodies. Cased
or overlay glass is covered with
one or more coloured outer
layers. Flashed glass has a colour
stained onto the outside, which is
then annealed to make the colour
permanent. The coloured layer is
engraved to show the glass body
underneath. This glass has been
overlaid with ruby glass and
engraved with a religious scene.
The foot is elaborately cut, an
indication of its quality.
* It is important to be able to
distinguish flashed from overlay
glass: flashed glass was usually a
less expensive substitute.

Famous 19thC craftsmen
Of the many artists who produced
good engraving, probably the
most sought-after are August
Böhm (1812–1890), Karl Pfohl
(dates unknown), Dominic
Biemann (1800–1857) and the
Pohls (dates unknown). Many
craftsmen travelled in Europe,
some came to Britain, and Böhm
even reached the United States.
* A few pieces are signed, and
can help identify unsigned wares.

Bohemian engraving can often be
identified by its subject: views of
German cities are an obvious
example. Other features are
heavy and ornate cutting, both on
the base and the sides of the
piece. This tumbler is a good
example with intricate cutting on
the base. The decoration is religious, featuring a monstrance (a
vessel in which the bread for
Communion is kept), and was
probably made for a priest.

J. & L. Lobmeyr
The Lobmeyr factory was founded by Josef Lobmeyr in 1822.
Towards the end of the 19thC his
sons Louis and Josef Jr helped to
revive past techniques. They produced *Schwarzlot*, enamelled and
rock crystal-style glass.

This heavily-cut jug in the
Baroque style from around 1880
is another very fine example of
the Lobmeyrs' work. Pieces by
Lobmeyr were sometimes signed,
but the signatures may be hard to
find and are often worked into
the pattern: this jug is signed
within the design on the foot.

19THC BOHEMIAN COLOURED GLASS

Bohemian engraved, ruby-stained goblet c.1850; ht 10¼ in (27.5cm); value code D

Identification checklist for 19thC Bohemian ruby-stained goblets
1. Is the colour rich and solid with a thin outer layer?
2. Is clear glass visible through the engraving?
3. If engraved, does the design feature Germanic motifs (see pp.44–45)?
4. Is the glass body heavy and high quality?
5. Is the piece free from chips and other damage?
6. Is the stem knopped?
7. Does the glass have an elaborate foot?

Coloured glass
In the 19thC three main methods were used to colour glass:
* the entire glass batch is coloured by the addition of a metal oxide; one of the most famous colours to be developed in Germany was Johann Kunckel's (c.1630–1750) *Rubinglas* or ruby glass, created using gold chloride.
* casing or overlay, where a clear glass body is covered with a coloured outer layer, giving a good double surface for cutting.
* the clear body is covered with a thin layer of colour, two methods are involved here, known as "flashing" and "staining".
All three techniques were used by Bohemian glassmakers.

Flashing and staining
* Staining involves the application of metal oxides to clear glass, by painting, or by dipping the item into the stain, firing it at a low temperature to fix the colour,

and then cutting or engraving. This process creates a rich, solid colour. The ruby red stain shown on the valuable goblet in the main picture was invented in 1832 by Friedrich Egermann (1777–1864), a glass blower and amateur decorator from northern Bohemia, using a mixture of gold and copper oxides. The engraved hunting scene on this piece is a typical Germanic motif. Bohemian goblets often featured knopped stems and elaborate feet.

* Flashing is a less expensive method of colouring glass, and involves the application of a very thin layer of molten coloured glass to a clear body. As the vessel cools, the layers fuse together.
* Flashed items were usually less expensive and tended to be made from lower quality materials than those that were stained.
* With the introduction of high quality metal oxides for colouring glass, some very intricate designs were produced.

Bohemian blue glass
Developed around 1826, the use of ultramarine in glassmaking was just one of many contributions made by the Bohemian glass industry during the 19thC. The shades vary from very pale blue to almost black.

These north Bohemian blue overlay vases from around 1860 were engraved by Franz Zach who was well known for producing blue-cased crystal pieces. He even attempted to produce a replica of the famous Roman cameo piece, the Portland Vase (see p.21) using this technique.

Other Bohemian coloured glass
Several exhibitions held in Prague in the 1820s and 30s stimulated an interest in glassware which led to the discovery of many different colours for glass including violet, pink and new shades of green and blue.

One of the most unusual new colours, discovered by Josef Riedel was a transparent yellow-green (*Annagrün*) and green-yellow (*Annagelb*) glass produced by adding small quantities of uranium to the batch.
* Uranium was also used to produce an opaque, apple-green glass, known as chrysoprase.
* As well as the ruby stain, Friedrich Egermann (see *above left*) produced a yellow stain from silver chloride, and an agate-like effect on glass called *Lithyalin* (see pp.40–41).

Collecting
* The quality of the colour, and overall condition are the main determinants of the value of 19thC Bohemian glassware.
* Feel the item carefully to detect any damage: often chips are less obvious on coloured glass.
* Look for damage to feet: ornate feet can easily be re-cut, but they will be smaller and may look out of proportion.
* Blue-stained Bohemian glass often fades; this can seriously affect value.
* Goblets were often made with covers; those with covers are worth 25 per cent more than those without.

FRENCH GLASS

St. Louis latticinio basket, c.1850

The history of the French glass industry dates from Roman times. Glassmaking was already a thriving industry in Rome, and as the Empire expanded, Roman glassmaking knowledge spread across Europe. By the late 1stC AD Pliny the Elder mentions glassworks in both Gaul (France) and Spain. With the decline of the Empire, Roman influence over French glass decreased and northern European glassmaking areas developed distinctive styles of their own.

Made from the ashes of ferns or bracken, the first French glass known as *verre de fougère* or forest glass, was amber or pale green in colour. It closely resembled German *waldglas*. Very little glass surviving from this time can be positively attributed because styles were primitive, copied from horn and wooden utensils, and did not constitute an identifiable national type.

The industry operated on a small scale until the Middle Ages when a demand arose for decorative glass windows; most were made for churches, but later for large houses. The technique of producing stained glass spread to France from the Byzantine churches of the Middle East, some of the best surviving examples can be seen at the Cathedral of St. Denis outside Paris. France also had an important role in the production of plain window glass with the establishment of a factory producing crown glass founded by Syrian glassworkers in Normandy.

Venetian forms exerted a strong influence on local glass production, and very little "French"-style glass was made during the period up to the 17thC. Small groups of *Façon de*

Venise goblets and opaque glass were made in France before this time, but are very difficult to distinguish from other Venetian-style wares.

A highly individual style originated at the beginning of the 18thC around the town of Nevers in central France, the site of a window glassworks since the early 17thC. Small figures of religious, social or historical significance made in lamp-blown glass were produced, often arranged in tableaux; the Nativity was one of the most common. Reasonably distinctive glasswares were also produced in Normandy, where small, light, wine glasses were made in the early 18thC, and also jugs made from good quality soda metal were exported to England. But, while changes in materials and techniques were occurring in other European glassmaking centres, the French industry in general continued to produce *verre de fougère* in styles with a Venetian influence.

A leap forward in design and manufacture occurred at the end of the 18thC possibly spurred on by the upheaval caused by the French Revolution, which began in 1789. The Compagnie des Cristalleries de Baccarat had been founded in 1765 and began producing lead crystal glass during the 1780s. Following the Battle of Waterloo in 1815 which marked the end of the Napoleonic Wars, European markets stabilized; this fact, allied to a protectionist economic policy in France, helped the Baccarat factory to become one of the major European glass manufacturers, producing an enormous range of top quality items, initially in an English style but later developing distinctive French forms. Baccarat cut glass often featured ormolu mounts and other gilded decoration. As well as pieces made from high quality lead metal, Baccarat produced *sulphides* which appeared as silvery-white inclusions, usually in the form of a portrait, inside clear and coloured glass. Enamelled crests were used in a similar way and were also very popular. Another characteristic Baccarat product was *verre opaline* – white or pastel-coloured opaque glass. Opaline pieces were usually beautifully-shaped and made in a classical style.

Another well-known French factory, the St. Louis Glassworks was also founded in the mid-18thC, and produced lead crystal from around the same time as Baccarat, but their styles were less influenced by their mainly Irish workers, and their wares were more distinctive from an earlier date.

All the main 19thC French glassworks made glass containing coloured canes. A decorative technique producing a mosaic effect, this was a refinement of earlier Venetian styles. The best-known examples of this form of decoration are seen in paperweights made by Baccarat, St. Louis and another famous factory, Clichy. These factories made a huge range in many different colours and styles, and are all extremely high quality. Made principally during the 1840s and 1850s, they are highly collectable, appear regularly at auction, and represent some of the most important French glass ever made.

18THC FRENCH GLASS

Verre de Nevers figures of an apostle, and a group of a knight on horseback c.18thC; ht 7½ in (19cm); value code C

Identification checklist for *Verre de Nevers* figures
1. Is the figure well modelled but unsophisticated, with a stiff posture?
2. Does it have an exaggerated facial expression?
3. Is the surface rough and dirty?
4. Is the figure a rustic subject?
5. If the piece is large, is it a figure and not an animal?
6. If a group of miniatures, do the figures comprise a pastoral scene?
7. Do there appear to be any pieces missing?
8. Is there a glass base?

Nevers (established 1603)
The glasshouse at Nevers is best known for its highly detailed figures made from opaque glass, produced by lampwork. This is a process in which glass is either blown or manipulated from clear or coloured rods over a torch or blow lamp. Common subjects include classical, comical, animal and religious figures. Similar pieces were also made in Marseilles, but Nevers has come to be used as a general term.

Verre de Nevers
The Nevers factory also produced miniatures, usually in groups depicting pastoral scenes. All *Verre de Nevers* figures are skilfully modelled but the poses tend to be stiff and unnatural, and the facial expressions tend to be exaggerated. The surface is rough to the touch and will therefore attract dirt.
* The delicacy of Nevers pieces means that they are often damaged, as is the apostle in the main

picture, which has lost two fingers from its right hand. Minor damage will affect the value of a piece, but will not render it worthless.
* If there is a group of figures make sure that none are missing – be suspicious of sets that are apparently incomplete.
* The figures usually have glass bases: the group in the main picture is standing on a base that resembles a patch of grass.
* If the surface of the glass is smooth and shiny, the piece is likely to have been made more recently.

Another famous glassmaking area was Normandy. Originally known for the manufacture of window or crown glass, it soon moved over to the production of table glass. Early 18thC Normandy glass has a Venetian influence, and this plain drinking glass with a fine metal, round funnel bowl and an inverted baluster stem, has a slight pink colour owing to natural impurities present in the mix.

Decoration
Pieces from later in the 18thC took on a style of their own, with quilted and wrythen (swirled vertical ribbing) decoration. Most decoration was carried out by hand "in front of the kiln", and moulding in a variety of styles was common. No cutting was used, and where pieces feature diamond point engraving, this was usually added at a later date.

Façon d'Angleterre
Towards the end of the 18thC some French glass was produced in a *Façon d'Angleterre* style, especially evident in some drinking glasses, and a group of engraved, tapering decanters.

French drinking glasses share some features of Dutch and British glass, such as folded feet, but belong to a distinct stylistic group. This glass has honeycomb decoration on the bowl and a conical foot with a folded rim. All this glass has a very rustic style and whilst it has a market in France, it is rarely seen in other European countries.

Decanters
French decanters can generally be distinguished from English ones because they are either much larger or smaller: the stan-

dard size for British decanters during this period was two imperial pints. Some French decanters were made in coloured glass, which is almost always blue, and have gilt and more rarely, enamelled decoration. This magnum decanter is particularly rare because it combines coloured glass with gilding and enamelling.

51

BACCARAT

A pair of Baccarat ormolu-mounted cut glass vases
c.1825; ht 22in (56cm); value code A

Identification checklist for 19thC Baccarat cut glass
1. Is the glass high quality lead crystal?
2. Is the cutting skilfully executed?
3. Does the piece appear unusually large?
4. Is it a particularly "French" style?
5. Does the piece have gilding, or gilt highlights?
6. Does it have gilt or ormolu mounts (silver is very rare)?
7. If there is a mark, does it appear on the mount rather than on the glass itself?

Baccarat (1765–present)
Baccarat, a French town in the north-eastern département of Meurthe-et-Moselle, is the site of the Compagnie des Cristalleries de Baccarat, founded in 1765. Production of cut lead crystal began in the 19thC. The two cut glass vases in the main picture,

with characteristic square, pillar-cut designs and ormolu (gilded bronze) mounting, are fine examples of world famous Baccarat craftsmanship.
* Known also for its paperweights (see pp.58–59), the firm remains one of the leading French glass manufacturers.

British lead crystal or Baccarat?

Baccarat benefited greatly not only from the introduction of British techniques of lead crystal production in France, but also from the employment of many Irish craftsmen. This has given rise to confusion over the identification of certain pieces: many by Baccarat have been wrongly attributed to British firms. Sometimes differences are obvious: the French used a good deal more gilded and ormolu decoration (silver mounts are very rare), some cut-glass designs are clearly not British, and items tend to be larger and heavier.

* When a piece cannot be positively identified, if it is made from high quality, well-crafted lead crystal, then whether it is British or by Baccarat, it will still command a premium.

The delicate shade of pink seen here on this large ice pail is a distinctive feature of many Baccarat wares. The characteristic gilt decoration and the gilt metal-mounted foot are also present. Classical decoration was popular among glass decorators of the time: the scene on this piece has been acid etched.

Marks

* Baccarat wares made from pressed glass, and those with ormolu mounts made before the end of the 19thC are marked simply with the name "Baccarat".
* Items with paper labels were made around 1900.
* Pieces with acid-stamped marks are almost all 20thC.
* An impressed butterfly on good quality pressed glass pieces is found on Baccarat glassware from the 1920s and 1930s.
* Anything marked "France" is modern.

Baccarat opaline glass

Pieces made from opaline glass formed another distinctive group of Baccarat wares.

The inventive form of this jug is typical of many Baccarat designs. The rim is decorated by a dark blue cane like those used in the production of the factory's beautiful paperweights. This method of embellishment was also used on small vases and dishes, and cabinet pieces such as this one are very sought after.

* Baccarat experimented widely during the 19thC and made tableware, lighting and furniture. Together with Val St. Lambert and St. Louis, Baccarat produced some of the earliest and best mechanically-pressed glass in Europe.

Baccarat rock crystal-style wares are characterized by their delicate form and heavy weight; this vase is typical. Baccarat first exhibited rock crystal engraving at the Paris Exhibition of 1878.

ST. LOUIS AND CLICHY

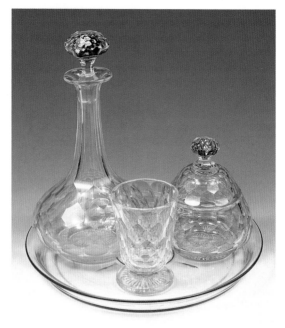

A St. Louis boudoir set, made from glass cut with honeycomb facets c.1850; ht 10½ in (27cm); value code D

Identification checklist for 19thC St. Louis glass crystal
1. If crystal, does the piece have a bright, high quality body?
2. Is it relatively heavy?
3. If the piece has a coloured base or stopper, does it feature *millefiori* or mosaic decoration?
4. Is the glass free from engraved decoration?

latticinio
1. If the piece has internal *latticinio* decoration, is it blue or pink, with white?
2. Is the rim finished with a glass cane?
3. Does it have a polished out pontil?

St. Louis (1867–present)
The glassworks at St. Louis (SL) in Lorraine produced clear crystal table wares from 1781, such as those in the main picture, often with "paperweight" or coloured cane style of decoration, on the stoppers of the bottles. This boudoir set was made for the bedroom, the decanter for water, a glass, and the small covered dish for sugar.
* A number of glasses and vases can be found with either *millefiori* (Italian for "a thousand flowers", a term used to describe mosaic

glass most commonly found in paperweights (see pp.58–59) stoppers or bases, and these are invariably SL. However, the factory is still producing similar items, and 20thC versions can be distinguished by the factory mark on the base.

Another typical form of SL decoration is *latticinio*, as seen on this small vase. The clear glass body is worked with canes of pink and white. The top of these pieces is often finished with a cane of the same colour (as in this case), or a contrasting one. The usual colours for this style of decoration are shades of pink or blue, and they nearly always include white.
* SL pieces with internal *latticinio* decoration always have a polished out pontil, and this distinguishes them from Venetian wares.
* Because they are made from crystal, SL pieces are relatively heavy.

Identification

SL made nearly all styles of tableware, but much of it is difficult to distinguish from the other great manufacturers of the period.

However, the majority of pieces are valuable and collectable because of their beauty and quality, and not because they can be positively identified. SL produced very little engraved glass, other than some pieces decorated with Bohemian-style hunting scenes, but a large amount of wonderful cut glass was made.
* Pieces that are identifiable include SL paperweights, and some overlay glassware including decanters, vases and large glasses.

This green-on-clear-glass gothic-style overlay decanter is typical.

Clichy

This glassworks, founded in 1837 by Joseph Maës at Billancourt, then moved to Clichy-la-Garenne, a Paris suburb. The factory produced mostly coloured

and overlay pieces and exhibited at many international trade fairs in the 1850s and 1860s. While being more famous for their paperweights, Clichy also made some *latticinio* items. They are usually less flamboyant than pieces by SL, such as this white decanter with red rim detail.

19THC FRENCH GLASS

A fine French enamelled and gilt mosque lamp, signed I. J. Imberton dated 1884; ht 12¼ in (32.5cm); value code C

Identification checklist for 19thC French opaline glass
1. Does the glass have a red and orange tint when held up to the light?
2. Is the piece decorative rather than useful?
3. Is the body delicate?
4. If enamelled, is the painting of a very high quality with very natural colours?
5. If enamelled, does the design feature realistic animal, bird or flower motifs?
6. Is there rubbed gilding around the rim and foot?

19thC French glass
Other than in the main factories, little table glass of real note was produced in France in the 19thC. Some artists and small factories, however, were producing interesting and often very beautiful items. The quality of French enamelling on glass was widely acclaimed at this time and artists received many commissions from abroad. When found today these pieces command high prices.

Islamic-style wares
Some of the best artists working in enamels included Philippe-Joseph Brocard and I. J. Imberton, who painted the mosque lamp in the main picture as part of a series made for customers in Egypt and Turkey. This lamp, a classic Islamic shape, decorated with gilt and enamel, features stylized motifs that were probably supplied by the person who commissioned it.

Philippe-Joseph Brocard (active 1867–90)

Brocard led the revival in Islamic glass enamelling, and was one of the most important artists during this period.

"Islamic" or Iznik-type wares, inspired by the brilliantly-coloured pottery produced at Iznik in Turkey in the 15th and 16thC, were popular in France at this time. Brocard signed his pieces with his surname, sometimes with the address of the firm, or "Brocard et Fils".
* Islamic style pieces are now rare and command high prices when they appear on the market. They are usually signed by the artist, but the factories where the glass bodies were made remain largely unknown.

Having first shown his work at the Paris Exposition of 1867 and been judged an innovator in this field, Brocard made this gilt and translucent enamel bowl for the London International Exhibition of 1871.

Other enamelled glass

Opaline or coloured opaque glass decorated with enamels was very popular in France in the 19thC. The white opaline ground was created by adding gold oxide to the glass mix; when an opaline piece is held up to the light, it is possible to see a red and orange tint, known as "fire".

usually older than those enamelled in the Islamic style, they will usually be worth only half as much.
* Vases are often gilded at the rim and on the foot; this often rubs away over time and cannot successfully be replaced.

Some of the most common opaline wares are vases, such as these, which were usually made in pairs. The quality varies enormously, but these vases, decorated with realistic birds and sprays of wild flowers in natural colours, are some of the best examples of glass painting during this period.
* Desirable painted subjects include exotic birds, animals and flowers; undesirable ones include more ordinary plants and figures.
* A single vase will be worth only a third of the value of a pair.
* Although opaline pieces are

A characteristic feature of French glass in the 18th and 19thC are metal mounts, usually made from gilt or ormolu (see pp.52–53), and these help to distinguish French wares from English or Bohemian pieces of a similar style. This enamelled, amethyst-tinted bowl, c.1850, is a typical, purely decorative piece. It has been drilled through the base to secure it to the square gilt pedestal mount: it would leak if filled with liquid.

PAPERWEIGHTS

A rare Baccarat close millefiori newel post dated 1884; ht 9½ in (25cm); value code A

Identification checklist for Baccarat *millefiori* weights
1. Does the piece feature densely-packed, stylized flower-head decoration?
2. Do some flower-heads include star or arrow-head motifs?
3. If the design includes silhouettes, are they birds or animals?
4. Is there an all-over carpet or "muslin" ground?
5. If marked, is there a letter "B" with a date: 1846, 1847, 1848 or 1849?
6. Is the glass free from bubbles and other imperfections?

Paperweights
The best and most widely collected paperweights were produced by the three French manufacturers, Baccarat, St. Louis and Clichy, during the 1840s. In the 1850s some French glassmakers emigrated to the United States, and important weights were made by the New England Glass Co., Boston & Sandwich Glass Co., and Mount Washington Glass Co. George Bacchus & Sons, Birmingham and Paul Ysart, Caithness made good British weights.

Technique

Paperweights are made using small sections of coloured glass rods or "canes", placed in a mould, and then set in clear, molten glass. Distinctive arrangements were used by each manufacturer which can help to identify the origin of a particular weight

Baccarat

Baccarat produced paperweights c.1845–c.1849. Many were made from clear crystal with canes cut to resemble the heads of tiny flowers. This densely-packed stylized flower decoration, known as *millefiori* ("thousand flowers") sometimes appeared with silhouettes of birds, animals, stars, arrowheads, and shamrocks. The silhouettes on the newel post (pedestal weight) in the main picture include a reindeer, swan, goat and butterfly. The all-over ground is known as "muslin". Sometimes a mark known as a "signature cane" appears; this one is "B1848". Other dates that appear include, 1846, 1847 and 1849, and are marked in red, green or blue on white canes.
* Other weights include a group made from clear and coloured glass set with silvery-white *sulphide* pictorial medallions.

St. Louis

St. Louis produced paperweights 1844–1850. A few weights are marked with dates between 1845 and 1849, but the most usual date is 1848. The reason is not known.

This weight features distinctive *latticinio* decoration (threads of glass arranged in a lattice design) often used by St. Louis. Many of their pieces were made with a *latticinio* ground, usually in white or pink. They tend to have higher domes than weights by Baccarat, and usually have star-cut bases.

* Other weights by St. Louis include large, single flower heads, such as dahlias and fuchsias, and hollow-blown crown weights with a cluster of twisted, ribbon canes.

Clichy

The best Clichy weights, produced 1846–1852, are never dated, and when signed rarely feature anything other than a "C" incorporated within the pattern.

Overlay weights, such as this one by Clichy, are rare because they were difficult and costly to make.
* Other forms of decoration favoured by Clichy include coloured swirls, and flower weights incorparting a small rose-shaped cane decoration that came to be known as the "Clichy rose".

Clichy weights were usually spherical, as shown here, with a flat, slightly concave base.
* Clichy weights are judged by many to be the best and tend to be the most expensive.

Collecting

* Size is important: most weights measure 2–4in (5–10cm) in diameter; unusual sizes, including miniature weights, with a diameter of.less than 2in (5cm), are highly sought after.

AMERICAN GLASS

Leaded glass window by Tiffany Studios, c.1910

Before the mid-18thC almost all American glass was imported from Britain and glass produced in the United States was
experimental. The impetus for domestic glass production
came following the American War of Independence
(1775–1777), when political ties with Britain were severed,
and British imports halted. Another stimulus came from Irish
and European immigrants, some of whom were skilled glassworkers. Many glasshouses were set up towards the end of
the 18thC, and items produced were a mixture of European
styles and designs. The most important of these were: the
Wistarburgh glassworks near Alloway, New Jersey, built by
Caspar Wistar (1692–1752); the glasshouse worked by Henry
William Stiegel (1729–1785) at Manheim, Pennsylvania; and
the New Bremen glassworks established by John Frederick
Amelung in Frederick County, Maryland, that was in operation for about ten years.

Early American glass included unrefined green glass
(Stiegel), bottles, window glass and colourless tableware
(Wistar), and English-style lead and non-lead stem and
tableware. Decoration included enamelling, cutting and

engraving. As well as producing tableware for everyday use, Amelung also made some commemorative engraved wares that are now highly sought after.

The style of American glass moved away from the largely Bohemian influence of the early 19thC, and after a brief "English" period went on to develop distinct forms and decorative techniques of its own. However, owing to the enormous home market, a large amount of glass was produced for functional, day-to-day use. As a result, apart from some special patents, such as Pyrex, relatively little American glass is found in Europe.

However, some American glass companies did develop entirely new and innovative techniques, such as mechanically-produced pressed glass, which revolutionized the mould-blowing technique. This process created pretty, decorative pieces, such as the Boston & Sandwich Glass Company's lacy glass, that was affordable so that glass was no longer a preserve of the wealthy. This innovation quickly found its way back to Europe, and pressed glass was soon being made in England, France and Germany.

The glassmaking areas of the US were largely unaffected by the American Civil War (1861–1865), but there were no further developments in styles or techniques. However the period of unity and stability following the war facilitated a comprehensive industrial revolution. Contact with Britain had been restored, and British glassmaking skills, finance and craftsmen were encouraged to come to the US and develop new companies. The most famous examples of British influence over the American industry are the glass-works of Steuben and Hawkes in Corning, Massachusetts. Both factories had British founders or senior designers who had been head-hunted in England, and who went on to produce some of the best and most "American" glass ever made.

Probably the most famous name associated with the glass industry in the United States is Tiffany. The Art Nouveau designs produced by Louis Comfort Tiffany in metal, jewelry and glass (and combinations of the three), are widely known and still copied throughout the world. Often "Tiffany" is used as a generic term describing a certain style, rather than a specific piece. Tiffany's father was a wealthy jeweler, and this gave him the chance to travel widely in Europe in his youth where he was influenced by the shapes and textures of ancient glass and early Art Nouveau. On his return to the United States he experimented with a variety of techniques and produced some highly distinctive wares, including lamps and vases.

Other American companies that produced collectable pieces include the Mount Washington Glass Co. (1837–1958) whose products include lamps, jugs, bowls and candlesticks in patented Burmese glass. The Steuben Glassworks produced some high quality, engraved crystal, Art Deco pieces including platters and stemware. The Boston & Sandwich Glass Co., the New England Glass Co. and the Washington Glass Co. all produced important paperweights.

AMERICAN PRESSED AND MOULD-BLOWN GLASS

Lacy, pressed glass compote, probably the Boston & Sandwich Glass Co. c.1835–1850; ht 5⅝ in (14.3cm); value code A

Identification checklist for early 19thC American pressed glass
1. Does the design appear quite sharp (softer patterns may be copies or European made)?
2. If coloured is the piece green, blue or amethyst?
3. Are seam lines visible on the body of the piece?
4. Does the piece have a rough pontil?
5. If the piece is a plate, does it have rough edges and a stippled background?

Pressed glass
The most important and influential innovation in 19thC American glassmaking was press moulding. Invented in the 1820s the process involved the use of a metal mould into which a gather of molten glass was placed. A plunger was used to force out any excess glass, and to press the glass down firmly onto the design on the walls of the mould. Between 1825 and 1830 12 press-moulded patents were taken out in the United States relating to a wide range of wares, including bottles and decanters. In 1864 the first patent was taken out for a steam-driven glass press.

This plate was designed to hold a tea cup while the tea was poured into the saucer to cool. Designs were often commemorative and frequently featured subjects or events connected with the locality of the glassworks.

* The major advantage of pressed glass was that items could be mass-produced at low cost, and this was later aided by increased automation.

* European press moulding is softer because the pattern was stretched. With the American technique, the pattern impressed onto the item is same size as the design inside the mould, and has sharper edges.

The Boston & Sandwich Glass Co. (1826–58)

The most famous manufacturer of pressed glass was the Boston & Sandwich Glass Co, founded by Deming Jarves. This company not only supplied the American home market, but exported wares to South America and the West Indies. The compote in the main picture is a typical example of their wares.

Lacy glass

Lacy glass is elaborate American pressed glass made to resemble embroidery. The lacy effect was created using a stippled (or beaded) background. Many different items in a huge variety of patterns were made using the pressed glass technique: the most common wares include water jugs and glasses, plates, candlesticks, and bases for oil lamps. Dolphins are a common motif and are often seen on the stems of candlesticks for example.

Collecting

* Although pressed glass is predominantly collected in the United States where it commands a premium, it is becoming more popular in Europe.

* Many exemplary pieces can be seen in American museums.

Mould-blown glass

A mould-blown glass is produced by enclosing a gather of glass in a hinged metal mould, the glass is blown until it fills the mould. If the mould features a design, this will appear on the outside of the vessel. Sometimes the seams of the mould are visible, caused by the heat of the glass expanding the mould until it is slightly open. This technique creates the effect of Anglo-Irish cut glass without the expense of the cutting process.

This mould-blown decanter has neck rings that were applied to the moulded bottle. Early pieces such as this had hand-finished details: neck rings on decanters, and handles on jugs. On later pieces all elements were formed in the mould.

* Mould-blown pieces can be distinguished from cut glass because the pattern can be felt on the inside as well as the outside of the item, and the finish is softer.

One of the best-known and comprehensively documented forms of mould-blown glass are flasks with impressed figures, made from around 1815, and popular throughout the 19thC. Many were purely for decoration, but others were made with political or patriotic subjects, such as presidential portraits, or for societies.

* Bottle-green or clear were the most common colours, but other shades of green, blue and amethyst are also found.

* Be wary of apparently rare examples, such as those commemorating obscure events, and famous politicians and soldiers, they may be copies.

TIFFANY

*A blue wisteria leaded glass and bronze table lamp, c.1906;
ht 27in (68.5cm); value code A*

Identification checklist for Tiffany lamps
1. Does the lamp have an Art Nouveau feel?
2. Does the ornamentation include naturalistic or floral motifs?
3. Does the piece have an organic, asymmetrical form?
4. Are the pieces of glass coloured and opaque with an iridescent surface?
5. Does the shade comprise hundreds of small pieces of glass?
6. Is there a small, marked tab on the inside of the shade?
7. Is there a number and a mark on the base?

**Louis Comfort Tiffany
(1848–1933)**
Son of the American jeweler Charles Tiffany, Louis Comfort travelled extensively in Europe and the Middle East in his youth where he became inspired by decorative styles and forms from many different countries. On his return to the United States he founded the Tiffany Glass &

Decorating Co. in 1892, and in 1902 he became art director of his father's company, Tiffany & Co. He designed a wide variety of decorative wares made from glass, including lamps, vases, screens and stained glass windows.

Many people commissioned Tiffany to decorate and to make pieces for their homes, including Mark Twain and Lily Langtry.

Tiffany's lamps

Tiffany began to produce lamps in around 1890. The shade was made from a large number of small pieces of his patented glass, *Favrile* (see *below*), within a bronze framework. The lamp bases, made from bronze or gilt bronze, were designed to resemble tree trunks.

The lamp in the main picture shows many typical features: a bronze, tree trunk base, an intricate shade comprising hundreds of pieces of coloured glass, and a naturalistic shape in an organic, asymmetrical style.
* There are many copies, but these tend to have fewer, larger pieces of glass.
* All Tiffany lamps carry a small copper tab on the inside of the shade, bearing the mark TIFFANY STUDIOS NEW YORK, sometimes with a number. This is often overlooked by forgers.

This *Favrile* vase has a characteristic elegant, naturalistic shape, with decoration carried out "in front of the kiln".

Cypriote

Tiffany used many methods to try and recreate the natural decay seen on the surface of glass that had been buried since ancient times. A variation of *Favrile*, *Cypriote* featured pitted, coloured, transparent yellow glass bodies that were rolled or marvered over crumbs of glass in blues, browns and greens, with a blue and purple iridescent sheen.

This leaded glass landscape window, c.1900, was commissioned by Howard Hinds for his Cleveland mansion.

Favrile

Inspired by Roman and Islamic glass, and originally called *Fabrile* ("hand made"), *Favrile* was patented in 1894. The glass was treated with metallic oxides and exposed to acid fumes.

This vase with a primitive form has an indented, swirled, metallic surface, characteristic of *Cypriote* glass.
* Apart from the heavily textured surface, *Cypriote* glass featured minimal hand-formed decoration.

OTHER AMERICAN GLASS

A pair of engraved and cut tazzas by T. G. Hawkes c.1890; ht 8in (20cm); value code D

Identification checklist for late 19thC designs by Thomas G. Hawkes
1. Does the piece have a heavy, well-made crystal body?
2. Is the decoration flamboyant?
3. If there is cut decoration, is it high quality and exceptionally bright?
4. Is the piece decorated with a "non-European" mixture of techniques (such as rock crystal engraving with bright cutting)?
5. Is there a "Hawkes" factory mark?

Thomas G. Hawkes & Co.
Towards the end of the 19thC there was a revival in the manufacture of cut glass in America: the growth of a wealthy middle class stimulated the production of more opulent wares. The pair of *tazzas* in the main picture, decorated in a typically flamboyant style, were made by the glass-cutting company T. G. Hawkes at Corning, New York state, c.1890.
* While the quality of the alternate cut and engraved panels seen on these *tazzas* is equal to European craftsmanship, it is rare to find both techniques on European piece.
* Later pieces have acid-stamped factory marks; earlier pieces occasionally have paper labels.

"Silver Deposit" glass
A decorative technique which first started in England, but was subsequently developed in the United States is the "Silver

Deposit" technique. First patented in Birmingham, England by Oscar Pierre Erard in 1889, it was later registered in the United

States by John H. Scharling in 1893. The high quality of this type of glass produced in the United States has meant it is now known as "American overlay".

A silver-rich mixture was applied to a glass body, fired and then buffed to create a rough surface. The item was then immersed in plating solution for several hours with a low electric current. The piece was then polished to a high silver finish. Some items, such as this scent flask were heavy enough to bear a silver mark, the stamp "sterling". In addition, silver mounts were often added, seen here *below left*. Silver deposit was used on almost every type of glass, including pressed glass, up until the First World War.

Steuben Glass Works (1903–present)
Steuben, one of the most famous American glassworks was founded by Frederick Carder (1864–1963), an Englishman, and Thomas Hawkes and family. Sent on a tour of American glassworks by his British employers Stevens & Williams, Carder met Hawkes,

and together Hawkes and Carder opened a factory in Corning in 1903. Carder was the company's Art Director for 30 years. Steuben produced a wide range of art glass and patented designs. The best known is *Aurene* ware produced between 1904 and 1933, such as the vase *above*, made c.1905–1920. *Aurene* pieces, most commonly vases, but dishes, table lamps and scent bottles were also made, usually have a blue and/or gold iridescent finish with a smooth, even surface.
* *Aurene* is usually marked on the base with an acid stamp featuring a fleur-de-lys and the word "Steuben" on a scroll.

* Other types of Steuben glass include *Calcite*, a plated glass with an *Aurene* finish on an opaque opalescent ground, made to simulate ivory, found on decorative wares and lampshades. *Cintra* featured a bubbled body with interior decoration, and *Verre de Soie* was a pale iridescent glass used to make stemware in the Venetian style.

Joseph Locke (1846–1936)
Another British glassmaker who came to prominence in the United States was Joseph Locke. Trained by the French engraver Alphonse Lechevrel, he worked at the glassworks of W. H., B. & J. Richardson, near Stourbridge in England and became interested in etching and acid decoration on glass. He produced fine cameo work for Richardson, including his version of the famous Roman cameo, the Portland Vase (see p.21). He moved to America in 1882 and was recruited by the New England Glass Company where he developed many techniques for acid decoration and colouring glass.

The acid-etched champagne glass c.1890 *below*, illustrates the characteristic complicated nature of Locke's designs. Often signed within the decoration, the signature appears towards the base of the bowl and reads "Locke Art".

* One of Locke's most famous inventions was *Amberina*, patented in 1883. This clear amber glass contained a small amount of gold in solution, and when sections of a vessel were reheated they changed to a rich, ruby red.
* Other patents include "plated *Amberina*" – opaque *Amberina*, and a stippled glass with blue and amber stains called *Pomona*.

OTHER GLASSMAKING AREAS

Red overlay, snowflake ground, bottle-form vase, China, c.18thC

Countries other than the main European centres also established their own glassmaking industries, and although in many areas styles were initially derivative, they developed their own techniques and designs. These areas tend to be characterized by their political and geographical isolation from the major European trading areas: Spain was separated by the Pyrenees; the Middle East by instability caused by the Crusades during the 11th–14thC and by hostile invaders such as the Moghuls; and Scandinavia, Russia, India and the Far East by physical distance.

The Middle Eastern glassmaking industry faltered after the fall of the Roman Empire. But the rise of Islam in the 7th and 8thC created a new identity and a rapidly growing market for all manufactured goods, including glass. Early Islamic glass was heavily influenced by Roman forms and decorative techniques but soon new styles developed and distinctive designs were produced. Many pieces were made for religious purposes, such as mosque lamps, many of which still exist. As glassmaking centres developed further west in France, Britain and Germany in the 17th and 18thC, the glass industry in the Middle East went into decline.

Glassmaking in India was first introduced by Mughal invaders in the 16thC; before this time there was no indigenous industry. The Mughals introduced Islamic styles and techniques, also seen in applied arts and architecture, but subsequently a distinctive "Indian" style developed. Other influences arrived in the 18th and 19thC when European-made glass was imported and decorated with enamels by local artists, and the wealthy preferred to buy foreign-made items. Styles of painting are very similar to that found in Mughal miniatures. Decoration tends to be more elaborate than Islamic glass, and figural subjects are common.

Glass was first produced in Spain when it became part of the Roman Empire. Wares derived from Roman forms were followed by those influenced by Moorish invaders. The isolated nature of the Spanish industry has meant that unusual styles and vessels have developed that are peculiar to Spain, and some of these items are still being made today.

In spite of an abundance of fuel in Scandinavia, there was no real glassmaking industry until the 15th–16thC, and as it became established it was mainly imitative, influenced by Venetian, Bohemian, and British forms. However, in the late 19thC some innovative designs and designers emerged, and their clean and dramatic styles have influenced all the great glassmaking centres throughout the world.

In 1634 the Tsar Michael of Russia authorized the production of glass. Gradually glassworks were established, centred around Moscow and St. Petersburg, many by the state or with the patronage of the Tsar or Tsarina, as much of the production was for the court. The most famous factory was the St. Petersburg Glassworks, later the Imperial St. Petersburg Glassworks, which produced Neo-Classical vases and urns, and tableware in an "international" style.

Glassmaking in China and Japan has never been a major industry. For Chinese craftsmen before the Qing Dynasty (1644–1912), the value of glass lay in its ability to imitate other materials such as jade, at a lower cost. Following his accession in 1661, the Manchu Emperor K'ang Hsi increased both the use and production of glass. Influenced by Jesuit missionaries especially from the Low Countries, he introduced Western techniques and forms. As the industry became more advanced a number of characteristic styles were produced: clear and opaque coloured glass has always been popular in China, and a bright, opaque yellow called "Imperial Yellow" was made exclusively for the court; opaque white glass painted in coloured enamels; a number of wares, including snuff bottles were produced in cased glass, usually a clear or "frosted" ground overlaid with red, blue or green, sometimes a number of different colours were used.

Although glassmaking first began in Japan c.7thC, the industry did not fully develop until the early 19thC when British representatives introduced European styles and technology. As well as producing imitative wares, such as cut-glass pieces, craftsmen also made toy glass trumpets, known as *pokon-pokon*, hair and comb ornaments, and *biidori-e* (glass plaques, often painted and engraved, set into furniture and walls). Important glassmaking areas include Nagasaki, Edo, Osaka, Satsuma, and more recently Tokyo.

SPANISH GLASS

A Spanish cántir, Catalonia
c.18thC; ht 12in (30cm); value code F

Identification checklist for 18thC Catalonian glass
1. Does the piece have an unusual form?
2. Is the piece relatively light in weight?
3. Does the piece feature coloured and applied decoration, such as trailing, milling or combing?
4. Is it free from cut and engraved decoration?
5. Are the edges smooth to the touch?
6. Does the glass include many small bubbles?
7. If clear, is the glass slightly grey in tone?

Spanish glass
A history of foreign invaders has meant that Spanish glass evolved from a mixture of Roman, Moorish and Venetian influences, and by the mid-18thC a number of highly distinctive forms had developed. The *cántir* (a two-spouted jug) in the main picture, evolved from a Middle Eastern vessel, and was made in Catalonia, in north-east Spain, one of the oldest and best-known glassmaking centres in the country. Other pieces unique to Spain include the *porrón* (a long-spouted wine vessel), the *jarrito* (a small, two-handled mug), and the *almorrataxa* (a four-spouted rose water sprinkler).

The two-handled vase *left*, with a honeycomb pattern was made in Granada in Andalucia, another major glass-producing region. Glass from this region tends to have an Arabic style, seen in Middle Eastern pottery and silver. Animal likenesses were not produced in this style because of the Moslem tradition. Pincered wings appear frequently on Spanish glassware.

The yellow-tinted glass oil lamp, *above left*, also from Catalonia shows a clear Roman and Venetian influence, seen in the blue trailed decoration, rib-moulded stem, and blue wings.
* Catalonian glass was made over a long period, and so the age of a particular piece can be difficult to determine. One guide is that earlier pieces tend to be lighter in weight.
* When collecting intricate pieces, feel for rough patches which could indicate chips.

Decoration
Spanish glass is usually quite elaborate, combining techniques such as coloured, trailed, combed, and applied decoration. Shapes or details in the form of animals are quite common: the piece in the main picture has a bird-shaped finial. Catalan and Andalucian glass is never cut or engraved. Gilded and enamelled decoration rarely appear. Clear Spanish glass, a soda metal made from the ash of the *barilla* plant, has a grey tint and contains many small bubbles.

La Granja de San Ildefonso
The most important Spanish glasshouse, La Granja de San Ildefonso was founded with Royal patronage near Madrid in 1728, originally to make window and mirror glass for the Royal family. After 1746. La Granja de San Ildefonso produced distinctive wares with strong Bohemian and Irish influences.

Pieces from La Granja de San Ildefonso were usually made from clear glass, occasionally from white or blue. They were the only Spanish wares to feature enamelling or engraving. Glasses and tumblers made at La Granja,

were often shallowly engraved and filled with gold which was fired at low temperatures, see *below left*. As the gold was not annealed onto the surface of the glass, it is therefore quite rare to

find the gilding in good condition. They are nearly always adorned with flowers, particularly roses. Tumblers were also decorated using coloured enamels, as seen on the glass pictured *above*.
* Another common flower found on tumblers from La Granja is the tulip, suggesting that some decorative glassware was made for export to the Low Countries.

MUGHAL AND INDIAN GLASS

A gilt and enamelled case bottle
c.19thC; ht 5in (13cm); value code A

Identification checklist for 17th–19thC Indian glass
1. Is the item made from clear glass (coloured pieces are unusual)?
2. Is the piece functional rather than purely decorative?
3. Does the piece feature gilded and/or enamelled decoration?
4. Is the decoration detailed and brightly coloured?
5. Is the design similar to the painting found on Indian miniatures?
6. Is the decoration in good condition?

Mughal and Indian glass
Glass was introduced to the Indian sub-continent by Islamic Mughal invaders who established the Muslim empire of India in c.1526, and continued to dominate the area until 1857. An Indo-Islamic style evolved from Persian art and architecture and this was absorbed into all the decorative arts, and much Indian glass features characteristic gilded and coloured enamelled decoration as seen on the flask in the main picture. A suspension of powdered gold leaf was used for gilding, and powdered glass, or frit, in paste form for enamelling.
* Most Mughal glass was made from the late 17th–mid-19thC.

European influence

During the 18th and 19thC, a number of glass items were made in Europe for the Indian market. The Indian nobility provided a healthy market for European manufacturers.

The square decanter in the main picture, possibly of Dutch origin, would have been part of a boxed set for spirit bottles. The gilded and enamelled design is based on an Indian miniature painting. The bright colours and detailed workmanship are typical of Indian tastes.

* Decoration often includes figures such as animals, plants and human forms, and is therefore distinguishable from Islamic glass which never features figures.
* Other countries produced pieces for sale in India – for example, cut glass hookah bases *right*, were manufactured in Ireland in the late 18thC.

Islamic influence

The Persian-Islamic influence over Mughal and Indian glass was considerable. From the 7thC onwards glassmaking flourished in the Middle East under Arabian Islamic rule. Forms and styles were based on techniques inherited from the Roman period: concave cutting, mould blowing and applied ornamentation. The most common forms of decoration were gilt, enamel and lustre.

This 12thC glass beaker also shows Roman-influenced Islamic decoration with spiral trailing and applied turquoise prunts.

Condition

Minor damage on early Indian glass is acceptable.

Hookah bases

One of the most common glass forms was the *huqqa* or hookah base, a globe-shaped bottle which was attached to a long, flexible tube and used for smoking.

The relief-cut "bull's eye" decoration *above* shows a clear Roman influence. Like much Islamic glass, this bowl from the 7th–8thC, is small and functional.
* Decoration on Islamic glass includes inscriptions, stylized patterns, occasionally flowers, but never figures.
* Middle Eastern Islamic glass is more restrained than glass from Spain (see pp.70–71) which was also part of the Islamic empire.

This hookah base is a good example of Islamic-influenced gilded and enamelled decoration: the stylized peacock feathers are typical of Persian and Mughal art. The spherical shape, however, is specific to Mughal glass, hookahs from other areas of Asia and the Middle East are bell shaped.
* Later Indian wares include flasks, sprinklers and spouted vessels.
* Although these pieces occasionally appear at auction houses, they are extremely rare and most are found in museums.

SCANDINAVIAN GLASS

Goblet by Kosta Boda, Sweden
c.1880; ht 8in (20cm); value code G

Identification checklist for 18th and 19thC Swedish drinking glasses
1. Is the body made from good quality lead crystal?
2. Is the bowl decorated with gilding or engraving?
3. If there is a monogram, is there also a crown (crowns are more common in Scandinavia than in the rest of Europe)?
4. Does the glass have a form similar to European styles?
5. Does it appear taller and narrower than its European counterparts?

Scandinavian glass
There is no record of glassmaking in Scandinavia until the mid-16thC, in spite of an abundance of forests to supply wood for fuel. There is archaeological evidence of a primitive glass industry from 1580–1650, and written records show that German glassworkers were employed at these factories producing window glass and tablewares. Records also show Venetian glassmakers worked in Stockholm and Copenhagen, but no attributable work exists.

Collecting
English and Scandinavian glass is similar; buying in Scandinavia will not guarantee authenticity because Scandinavian glass is rarer than British glass.

Sweden
The earliest identifiable Scandinavian glass comes from a factory at Kungsholm Glasbruk in Sweden, founded in 1686 by a Muranese glassworker called Giacomo Bernadini Scapitta and remained active until 1815.

The factory also produced some tall, thinly-blown *Façon de Venise* goblets, such as the one *above*, with unusual stems and decorated with crowns and monograms for royal patrons, including a set made for Charles XI of Sweden (1660–1697). They were made with covers but few of these have survived.

German influence
By the mid-18thC the Germanic style had become dominant. Two main factories produced this style of wares. First, Skånska Glasbruket at Henrikstorp in Scania (1691–1760) which made rustic-style engraved glass, and Göteborg Glasbruk, Gothenburg (1761–1808), which pioneered the production of Scandinavian cut, coloured glass, especially deep blue and opaque white.

Kosta Boda (established 1742)
Sweden's oldest surviving glasshouse is the Kosta Boda factory in Småland, the site of a great deal of more primitive glassmaking. Kosta employed foreign workers throughout the 18th and 19thC. They made wares that are difficult to distinguish from similar styles produced elsewhere in Europe. The Biedermeier-style goblet in the main picture is signed and can therefore be positively identified; it was made around 1880. Biedermeier wares were originally produced in the 1840s (see pp.40–41).

Norway and Denmark
From 1397–1814 Norway and Denmark were a single nation with the capital based in Copenhagen. There is no evidence of glassmaking before the founding of a glassworks at Nöstetangen in Drammen, Norway in 1741, by an army officer called Caspar Herman von Storm. Originally staffed by only German workers, von Storm was quick to respond to changes that were occurring elsewhere in Europe and encouraged two British glassworkers, James Keith and William Brown from Newcastle-upon-Tyne, to work for him.

Keith introduced the Anglo-Venetian form to Norway, as seen in the engraved wine glass *above*, and some popular 18thC stem forms, including the baluster, and the air and opaque twist.
* These glasses can be easily distinguished from British pieces: the bowls are larger with greyer metal, often with Germanic-style heraldic engraving.
* The glassworks at Nöstetangen produced all forms of glassware, including three chandeliers designed by the Silesian craftsman Heinrich Gottlieb Köhler, who was also famous for his engraving, and blown by James Keith in blue and red crystal.

Late 19thC Scandinavian glass
The late 19thC was a period of change and modernization; many forms were adopted from other areas. Production was high quality, but styles are not distinctive enough to facilitate identification without a signature or mark.

RUSSIAN, CHINESE AND JAPANESE GLASS

Enamelled glass from the Russian Imperial Manufactory, St. Petersburg shown at the International Exhibition, London, 1862

* An identification checklist for Russian, Chinese and Japanese glass would be inappropriate because of the variety of forms and styles produced.

Russian glass

Glass was manufactured in Russia only on a small scale before the late 17th and early 18thC, when a number of state-sponsored glass-works were established, most notably the St. Petersburg Glassworks (later the St. Petersburg Imperial Glassworks) in 1777. The factory produced a variety of wares, including the examples of gilded and enam-elled glass seen in the print in the main picture. Also produced were enamelled beakers and engraved, monogrammed *pokale* or goblets.

Tsarina goblets

Some of the best-known pieces of Russian glass are Tsarina goblets. First commissioned by the Empress Elizabeth Petrovna (1741–1761) and Catherine the Great (1762–1796), they are often engraved and inscribed with Imperial symbols.
* It is believed that there was a considerable German influence in the production of these glasses – many workers from Saxony were employed in Russian glasshouses during this period.

This baluster-style goblet from c.1750 is engraved with a bust of Elizabeth Petrovna, and the Imperial eagle and cypher.
* Russian glassworks in the 18th and 19thC produced many items made from cut-crystal glass in a European style, including chandeliers and other tableware such as wine glass coolers.
* Glass produced in southern areas of Russia from around 1894

was made in the Moslem style, decorated with thick gilding and enamelling.

Chinese glass
Glass made in China dates from the reign of the Manchu Emperor K'ang Hsi (1661–1727) who was influenced by Western missionaries. A variety of glass wares were then produced including plain and coloured clear and opaque glass, carved and overlay glass, and white enamelled glass made to imitate porcelain.

Chinese Overlay glass
The best known Chinese glass are cameo pieces with a coloured overlay and opaque white ground. Made to resemble precious stones, carving is distinctly oriental in style.

Initially red and clear or "snowflake" white were more commonly used for Chinese overlay wares. Other colour combinations soon became popular, such as this blue and white jar and cover from the 19thC which imitated blue and white Chinese porcelain, and even multi-coloured overlay or "marquetry".

Coloured glass
Many types of plain and coloured glass were produced in China, and were popular because of their resemblance to the colours of precious stones and mineral deposits. Blue glass was popular because it resembled lapis lazuli, and red and yellow glass was favoured because it looked like realgar, a mineral containing arsenic.

Possibly the most well-known single colour among Chinese glass is "imperial yellow" which echoed the yellow-glazed porcelain used exclusively by the Emperor and his family. This carved Peking vase from the mid-18thC, illustrates the characteristic rich, egg-yolk yellow.

Collecting
* Chinese glass is still made by hand, so be careful – it can be difficult to distinguish between old and new wares.
* The value of Chinese glass is determined more by quality than age. Wear is not a reliable indicator of age because many pieces were made simply for display.
* Copying in China is considered to be a mark of respect – even down to signatures and marks: take care when evaluating any piece.

Japanese glass
Glass was made only sporadically in Japan before the late 18thC, and was mainly used to make beads, but in the early 19thC the British introduced lead crystal glassware, and especially cut glass, into the country. Japanese craftsmen copied the designs and became increasingly skilled, and soon glass began to be used to make traditional Japanese items such as *biidori-e* (glass inlay found in items such as trays and furniture), *inro* (small boxes) and *netsuke* (miniature carvings), although it never became as popular as lacquer, wood or ivory. Other types of glass include mirrors, lamps, clear and coloured cut glass, and plate glass.

ENGLISH DRINKING GLASSES

A double series opaque twist ale glass, gilded with hops and barley, c.1760

Apart from some evidence of Roman glassmaking and a small amount of medieval "forest" glass made in the Weald area of southern England, virtually no glass was produced in Britain before the late 16thC, all supplies were imported.

In 1567 Jean Carré a glassmaker from the Low Countries was granted a licence to make window glass and other wares at Alford in Sussex. Progress was slow, and in 1570 Carré opened a glassworks at Crutched Friars in London, keen to bring the techniques of *Façon de Venise* to Great Britain. He brought over a number of Italian craftsmen from Antwerp, including the Muranese glassworker, Giacomo Verzelini (1522–1606) who had lived and worked in Antwerp for 20 years. Verzelini became manager, and following Carré's death in 1572, acquired a licence to produce Venetian-style glass, and the government prohibited the import of glass from Venice for the next 21 years. There are still about 12 identifiable Verzelini pieces in existence, mostly in public collections. They are usually diamond-point engraved, and often include a cartouche with a shield, a quotation, a dedication or a date. After Verzelini's retirement in 1592, the remaining years of his patent were granted to Sir Jerome Bowes, a soldier. And in 1618 Sir Robert Mansell, a retired admiral and financier obtained control of the national monopoly. Under Mansell the glass industry produced a wide range of utilitarian wares including wine and medicine bottles, and good quality drinking vessels. The government policy of creating a monopoly in the glass industry lapsed in the mid-17thC.

The most significant development in British glassmaking occurred in 1675, when the Glass Sellers Company employed George Ravenscroft (1632–1683) to research the production of a new form of glass that, unlike Venetian *cristallo*, was not vulnerable to surface cracks, or crizzling. By 1677, Ravenscroft's formula had proved successful enough to be granted a patent. His mix contained a relatively high proportion of lead oxide, between 24 and 30 per cent, and became known as flint or lead crystal. Some of his early pieces were marked with his seal, a raven's head. Lead glass was more brilliant than *cristallo* (see pp.22–23), and was softer and therefore better suited to cutting and engraving.

From the late 17thC British glass developed its own shapes and styles that set the standard for table glass throughout the world for the next 100 years. Early 18thC lead glass tended to be very heavy, but in 1745 an Excise Act levied a tax on glass at the rate of 1d (one old penny) per pound of raw materials. As well as a means of generating revenue, it was also hoped that the tax would encourage manfacturers to reuse pieces of old glass (or cullet) in the mix, which lowered the melting point and used less fuel. This left more wood available for boat-building and other uses. As a result, lighter styles of glassware developed, illustrated by stems with tears, twists and facets found on many 18thC drinking glasses.

Drinking glasses made during this period can be dated reasonably accurately by their stems. The first distinctive British form was the baluster; plain, heavy balusters with knopped stems based on a Renaissance architectural form, were made between 1685 and 1725. Lighter glasses known as balustroids, and glasses with plain stems were produced from 1725–1750. Moulded pedestal or Silesian stemmed glasses can be dated between 1715 and 1760. Other popular stems included the following: air twists made between 1745 and 1770; opaque or cotton twists between 1755 and 1785; and faceted and rudimentary (very short) stems between 1780 and 1825.

In 1777 the glass tax in England was doubled and extended to include coloured glass, which even affected the production of opaque glass. When this was followed three years later by the granting of free trade to Ireland where the glassmakers had previously been banned from exporting their wares, many English glassmakers moved to Ireland to escape high costs. The industry flourished, and a characteristic, high quality, heavily cut style emerged.

*An Anglo-Dutch armorial goblet
c.1685; ht 7¼ in (18.5cm); value code B*

Identification checklist for 17thC Anglo-Dutch glass
1. Is the glass body very thin?
2. Does the glass appear slightly smoky in tone and (probably) crizzled?
3. Has the stem a spontaneous appearance reflecting the free-blown glass-making technique?
4. Does the glass have a flat foot?
5. If decorated, is the piece engraved?
6. If engraved, is there very little depth to the cutting?
7. If the decoration is armorial, is there a full coat of arms rather than simply a crest?

Anglo-Dutch and Anglo-Venetian glass
Drinking glasses found in Britain before c.1690 were heavily influenced by Venetian and Dutch styles but were usually of inferior quality. Although contemporary documentation does exist it is unclear whether many early 17thC glasses were made in Venice or Holland for sale in England, or whether they were manufactured in England in imitation of fashionable foreign styles. Drinking glasses of this type are therefore generally classified as Anglo-Dutch or Anglo-Venetian.

Nearly all have a "crizzled" surface: a milky, cracked appearance due to small fissures in the surface which allow water to infiltrate the metal of the glass.

Anglo-Dutch glass

The Anglo-Dutch armorial goblet in the main picture is made from typically crizzled lead glass. This is one of a group of glasses thought to have been engraved by Dutch makers in Holland using Venetian glass-making techniques. Despite their evident imperfections, glasses such as this were a luxury and, as seen here, were usually elaborately diamond point engraved. The status of such pieces is also reflected in the fact that most are decorated with coats of arms. This one has the arms of William of Orange as Stadholder of the Netherlands (before he became William III).

Styles

Although the moulding on the base of the bowl and multi-knopped stem is very typical of Venetian glass of the 17thC, the flat foot is characteristic of Anglo-Dutch glass. True Venetian glasses have more conical-shaped feet. The hollow stem was free-blown and because the soda glass used cools relatively quickly the design has a visible spontaneity.

Anglo-Venetian glass

Most 17thC Anglo-Venetian glass has a simpler shape and style than seen in Dutch examples.

These glasses also have distinctive, high conical feet.
* Anglo-Venetian glasses are not often engraved and any decoration is usually purely decorative,

rather than having any political and social significance.
* Like Anglo-Dutch glass, Anglo-Venetian glass was made from soda glass although most contain some lead. All glasses of this type therefore feel surprisingly light.

Value

Although all 17thC glass was a luxury, according to contemporary records of imports, Anglo-Venetian glasses were originally more readily available and cost a fraction of the price of the more elaborate Anglo-Dutch glasses. They were employed in affluent households for everyday use. Although nowadays such pieces are as rare as Anglo-Dutch glasses they are worth rather less.

Decoration

Engraved decoration on both Anglo-Dutch and Anglo Venetian glass was carried out using a diamond point stylus because the thin metal or glass body was too delicate to be wheel engraved. The design is scratched on to the surface of the glass freehand.

There is therefore typically little depth to the design and the individual scratch marks should be visible, as on this Anglo-Dutch goblet from around 1680.

Condition

Common to all British glass, condition needs to be perfect for a piece to be particularly valuable, however these glasses are so fragile they are rarely seen in perfect condition and repairs are usually easy to spot.
* Severe crizzling causes the top surface to flake and leads to the progressive deterioration of the glass, so avoid pieces that are badly affected.

HEAVY BALUSTERS

Heavy baluster with a mushroom knop c.1700; ht 6½ in (16.5cm); value code C

Identification checklist for heavy baluster glasses
1. Does the glass feel relatively heavy?
2. Does it have a slightly grey tone?
3. Is the base of the bowl very thick?
4. Is the foot conical or domed with a deep fold?
5. Does the stem have large, plain, well-defined knops?
6. Do the foot and bowl ring clearly when tapped?
7. Does the glass have a conical or funnel bowl (other shapes are more unusual)?
8. Is the glass free from decoration (engraving is rare)?
9. Is the surface free from crizzling?

Early 18thC drinking glasses
The development of lead crystal glass at the end of the 17thC meant that the British glass industry began to flourish in its own right and was no longer dependent on imported items and materials. It also marked the end of Venetian influence on the style of British glassware. Drinking glasses took on the baluster form that was already familiar on silverware and furniture, and there was an emphasis on strength and simplicity.

Heavy balusters
Glasses known as heavy balusters were produced between 1685 and 1710.
* The lead content of the glass mix means that they will feel very heavy, and will also give the glass a soft, grey tint. The surface

of early lead crystal glass is sometimes "crizzled" (see pp.80–81).
* Heavy balusters are usually made in three pieces: bowl, stem and foot. The base of the bowl is solid and adds to the overall weight of the glass.
* The foot is usually conical (sometimes domed) with a fairly deep fold for greater strength.
* The knops on heavy balusters are large, plain and well-defined. The first knopped stem form was the inverted baluster (c.1690), followed by the true baluster which has its most dominant knop at the base of the stem.

* The value of a heavy baluster is determined by the rarity of the shape of the knop: the acorn is the rarest and most valuable.

Usually heavy balusters measure between 6 and 8in (15–20cm), but there is a group of extremely large balusters. This mammoth baluster goblet, 12in (30.5cm), has a much larger capacity than is usual. Glasses such as these were probably made for special occasions and are rarely decorated.
* Size is not an advantage in terms of value: smaller pieces will always fetch a higher amount than larger ones, although the prices of larger glasses have recently been increasing.

Decoration
Heavy balusters were designed to stand as quality craftsmanship in their own right and so moulded and engraved decoration is extremely rare. Decorated pieces are very valuable.
* Some were engraved with names, initials, mottos or inscriptions, and a few were wheel or diamond-point engraved for commemorative reasons, but this decoration was always added later.

This fine baluster goblet from around 1710 shows all the features of the heavy baluster. The conical bowl has a solid tapering base, the stem has a dominant angular knop and a basal knop, and the foot is conical and folded. Bowls are usually conical and funnel-shaped; bell and thistle forms are less common.
* Heavy balusters were often recycled following the imposition of the 1745 Excise Tax; the large amount of glass that they contained meant they were often melted down to make more fashionable items. This has contributed to their rarity.

Knops
The knops on heavy balusters were plain at first, but by 1725 a number of more elaborate forms had developed including cylinder, ball, acorn, angular, bobbin, drop, mushroom and annulated (see pp.102–103).

Types of baluster glasses
Although all baluster glasses are rare, the largest proportion of these are goblets, but there are a number of cordial glasses with true baluster stems. Ale glasses, gins and drams are extremely unusual.

LIGHT BALUSTERS AND BALUSTROIDS

A rare Dutch stipple-engraved goblet by Frans Greenwood signed and dated 1745; ht 10in (25cm); value code A

Identification checklist for light balusters and balustroids

1. Is the stem longer than those found on heavy balusters (see pp.82–83)?
2. Does the piece weigh less than a heavy baluster?
3. Are the knops more complex and widely-spaced?
4. Is the base of the bowl thinner than on heavy balusters?
5. Is the piece elegant and well-proportioned?
6. If there is engraving, does it feature a Dutch subject?
7. If stipple engraved, is the glass signed on the pontil?

Light Balusters
Lighter baluster glasses were made in the first quarter of the 18thC even before the imposition of the Excise Act, as craftsmen became more experienced and were able to manipulate lead crystal with greater skill and ease. They are characterized by a wider variety of bowl shapes, including

bell, thistle and trumpet, and longer, more complex stems with smaller, lighter and less defined knop shapes.

This large baluster goblet (9in, 23.5cm) is from around 1720. Its stem is longer than those found on heavy balusters and the base of the bowl is no longer solid. It has a multi-knopped stem including double and triple-annulated knops above a domed foot.

Balustroids
"Balustroids" are glasses made in the baluster form after c.1725. More elegant than balusters, their stems are taller and thinner.

Balustroids have fewer, more delicate knops often separated by lengths of plain stem, seen here on this example c.1740.

Decoration
Decoration on light balusters and balustroids, as on heavy balusters, is rare. A few pieces are engraved, usually with designs reflecting the use of the glass – for example, grapes and vines for a wine glass, hops and barley for an ale glass, and apples for a cider glass. Commemorative engraving should again give cause for suspicion (see p.83).

Newcastle Light Balusters
An extremely sought-after group of balustroid glasses is the Newcastle Light Balusters.

These represent the highest quality of balustroids, and always have stems that are an inch or so longer than usual (approximately 7½in, 19cm), with exceptionally delicate knops, and conical feet that are often folded. They are frequently engraved – plain examples are very rare – and were popularly supposed to have been shipped from Newcastle to Holland for decoration by skilled craftsmen, but now it is thought that they were made in Holland by British manufacturers and then engraved by the best Dutch artists using diamond-point, wheel and stipple techniques.
* Common subjects include Dutch family crests, seen *above*, ships which were symbols of good luck, and drinking scenes.
* Stipple engraved glasses are often signed on the pontil (raised mark left on the base where the pontil rod is snapped off).

MOULDED-PEDESTAL
(SILESIAN) STEMS

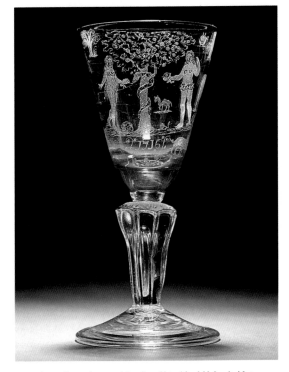

A rare diamond-engraved Royalist goblet, with a folded conical foot
c.1716; ht 8¼in (20.8cm); value code A

Identification checklist for Silesian-stem drinking glasses
1. Does the glass have a moulded pedestal stem with four, six or eight sides?
2. Does it have a conical bowl and foot?
3. If engraved, is the design a diamond-point engraved Dutch subject?
4. Does the glass feel relatively heavy?
5. Do both the foot and the bowl ring when tapped?
6. Does the metal have a grey tone?
7. Is the stem solid, perhaps with a small tear?

Silesian-style stems
Dated between 1710 and 1750, and therefore earlier than some balusters and balustroids, Silesian stems became popular following the accession of the Hanoverian George I in 1714. This particular moulded pedestal form originated in Silesia, one of the glass-making centres in central Europe, then part of Bohemia and now part of Poland, but these glasses have no actual link with the area. Relatively plain at first, the moulded shape gradually became more decorative.

Commemorative pieces

The glass in the main picture is a diamond engraved goblet with an octagonal moulded pedestal stem. Moulded on the shoulders of the stem are the words "GOD SAVE KING GEORGE", an inscription referring to George I. The typically English engraving depicts "The Fall of Man", a popular decorative subject at that time. This goblet is particularly rare because it is the only example of a combination of what is probably a marriage goblet, with a Royalist theme.
* Even though English engraving is cruder than Dutch, it is rarer and therefore more valuable.

This glass has a domed panel-moulded foot that is usually found on sweetmeat glasses designed to sit on top of *tazzas*. This is very rare and probably adds around 25 per cent to the market value. The funnel bowl features a Dutch-engraved diamond point whale-hunting scene; glasses such as this were usually presented for good luck.

Tazzas

The commonest example of Silesian stem is found on *tazzas*, or flat raised salvers used to present desserts after a meal. They were made throughout the 18thC, and although pieces produced later in the century tend to be heavier and less refined, the style changed little during this time.

This tier of *tazzas* shows how they often formed a decorative focus. They are usually less expensive than Silesian-stemmed drinking glasses, and are quite difficult to date accurately.

English or Continental?

Silesian stems were made both in England and on the Continent; it is important to be able to distinguish between these different types because Continental Silesians are worth only half as much as English-made examples.
* English Silesian stems were made from lead crystal, the foot and bowl were free blown, and the stem was mould blown. The earliest and most valuable glasses have four-sided stems. Moulded stems with six and eight sides were produced later and are less valuable. Some stems were made with odd numbers of sides, but these were probably produced by mistake. Silesian stems typically have a conical bowl, a conical folded foot, and feel relatively heavy.
* Continental Silesian stems were made from soda glass, and therefore differ from their English counterparts in the following ways:
* the metal has a duller tone
* the foot and bowl do not ring when tapped
* they feel light in weight
* the stems are hollow, which adds to the weight disparity caused by the difference in the metal used.

PLAIN AND RUDIMENTARY STEMS

Large plain stem with engraved decoration and a drawn trumpet bowl c.1740; 8in (20cm); value code E.

Identification checklist for plain stems
1. If the glass has a plain stem, does it have a drawn trumpet bowl (other shapes were less common)?
2. Is the stem tapered?
3. Does it have a tear (stems without tears are less desirable)?
4. Is the foot conical and folded (although folded feet disappeared around 1745)?
5. If decorated, is it moulded or crudely engraved with motifs such as flowers, hops and barley, or fruiting vines?
6. Is the pontil snapped off (see p.85)?

Plain stem glasses
Glasses with plain stems were made alongside the more decorative balustroid between 1730 and 1760; they were less expensive and designed for everyday use. The glass in the main picture shows the typical features of a plain stem: the trumpet bowl (40 per cent were made with this type of bowl), and a folded foot which helped protect against chipping (less common after 1745). Another common feature was a tapered stem with a tear, usually near the bowl. Plain

stems with a drawn bowl shape were made in two pieces, those with other bowl shapes were generally made in three pieces, with a join visible between the base of the bowl and the stem.

This rare plain stem mead glass shows the distinctive cup-shaped bowl peculiar to mead glasses. Plain stems were also used for wine and beer.
* Decoration on plain stems included engraving (fruiting vines, flowers, hops and barley) and moulded patterns.

Rudimentary stems
Throughout the 18thC many small glasses were made with very short stems, or bowls set directly on the foot. Known as rudimentary stems, they were less expensive glasses, made for taverns and everyday use.

Ale glasses were made with rudimentary stems of all types. They are usually 4–5in (10.2–12.7cm) tall with a conical bowl. There are two main forms of decoration: first, "wrythen" moulding, formed by twisting vertical ribbing to give a spiral effect, the

dwarf ale glass c.1770 *below left*, has been "half-wrythen"; second, engraved with hops and barley.

Jellies
Foods such as calf's foot jelly, savoury and other jellies, were popular during the 18thC. The glasses they were eaten from have come to known as "jellies".

This typical plain jelly glass has a flared rim and a short stem with a bladed knop. The bowls are usually about 4in (10.2cm) high, and frequently found shapes include, pan-topped, bell, round funnel, cup, and sometimes hexagonal. The most common form of decoration is moulding on the bowl; some jellies have handles.
* If a jelly has only one handle it is possible that the second has been lost: look out for recutting.

Drams are found with all 18thC stem forms, and were generally small, inexpensive glasses used in taverns to serve spirits such as gin and brandy. Bowl shapes vary enormously – this dram has a barrel bowl, stems are short and simple, and they have conical feet which were folded before 1750, and may be uneven.
* Forms of decoration include crude engraving, moulding on the bowl and knopped stems.

An engraved air twist wine glass with a central collar
c.1750; ht 6½ in (16.5cm); value code E

Identification checklist for early 18thC air twist glasses

1. Is the bowl trumpet-shaped (other forms are more unusual)?
2. Does the twist extend into the base of the bowl?
3. Is the twist inside the stem?
4. Is the foot folded?
5. Is the pontil snapped off?
6. If engraved, does the decoration feature an armorial, commemorative, convivial or political design?
7. Is the twist neat and well formed?
8. Is the glass good quality lead crystal?

Air twist stems

Air twist stemmed glasses proliferated between 1750 and 1760, as craftsmen sought to find a way to produce drinking glasses that were both light in weight and sufficiently decorative to have consumer appeal. Early air twists, such as the glass in the main picture, were made in two pieces, with the twist extending into the bowl. The bell bowl seen here is unusual, most early air twist glasses had drawn trumpet bowls.

Technique
Air twists were formed by denting a gather of molten glass, and placing another gather on top, thereby creating air bubbles, and then elongating and twisting the pattern made by the air by drawing and rotating the molten glass until it assumed the length and breadth needed for a stem.

The most simple form is the multi-spiral air twist, seen in the main picture, which may contain up to 12 filaments. A stem with only one style of twist is known as a single series air twist. The glass *above* has a double series air twist stem, with two different styles of twist: a pair of corkscrew twists outside a vertical cable.
* A rare stem form, the mercury twist has flat rather than round threads, and the increase in the reflective surface gives a "quicksilver" effect.

Decoration
Air twists sometimes feature English diamond point engraving which varies greatly in quality. The subjects are commemorative, armorial, convivial or political, such as the Jacobite design (see pp.96–97) on the glass in the main picture.
* Some air twists were made with knops. This is a very skilled process and knopped air twists are rare: one knop may add 20 per cent to the value of a glass, and up to five can be found on a stem.

Copies
Copies have been made since 1850, and those made later have ground-out pontils (on original air twists the pontil is snapped off) and flatter feet. Many were made

with over-bright metal and have a white tone. They have a slightly clumsy feel, and they are often larger than 18thC originals. Many later copies had factory marks, but these are sometimes removed by less honest dealers.

Some contemporary 18thC glasses are made of soda metal. Soda glass cools relatively quickly which means that work has to be done faster, and twists are invariably not so good. The glass on the left *above*, is an English, lead crystal air twist, with a neat, well formed, double series twist; the glass on the right is made from Dutch soda metal, and has an irregular and unattractive twist.

Incised twists
The incised twist was a stem form made to imitate the air twist with spiral or wrythen moulding on the outside of the stem.

This incised twist has a typical round funnel bowl, a shape that was about five times more common than any other. However, a group from the North of England were made of soda metal, and these always have waisted bell bowls and folded feet.

TWISTED STEMS II

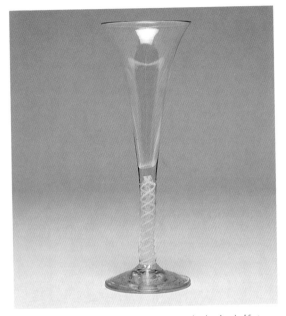

Double series opaque twist with a drawn trumpet bowl and conical foot c.1770; ht 7½ in (19cm); value code F

Identification checklist for 18thC colour twists
1. Is a join visible at both ends of the stem?
2. Are the twists solid and well formed?
3. Do the colours include green and/or red (blue and yellow are unusual)?
4. Is there also an opaque twist in the stem?
5. Does the bowl have a grey tint?
6. Is the bowl free from engraved decoration?
7. Does the glass ring when tapped?
8. Does it feel relatively heavy?

Opaque twists
Opaque or cotton twists date from 1760–1780 and are probably the most collected and easily recognizable stem form of all English 18thC drinking glasses. This form of decoration owes much to the Venetian *latticinio* and *vetro di trino* techniques of the early 17thC, where threads of white were enclosed inside clear glass. The glass in the main picture is a typical example with a double series twist: virtually half of all opaque twists made were double series.

Technique
Opaque white glass is formed using tin oxide. The twist was made by taking a gather of clear glass, inserting rods of white glass, and pulling and twisting a length which was then cut into sections suitable for stems. The resulting white filaments could be drawn out until they were as fine as cotton threads. Opaque twists were made in three pieces: the foot and bowl were moulded to opposite ends of a pre-cut stem, and a join is visible at either end of the stem.

Coloured Twists

Colour twists are rarer than opaque ones because coloured enamels made with different metal oxides cool at different rates, thereby making the technique more complex. The most common colours are red and green, while blue and yellow are very rare.

* Colour twists usually appear with an opaque twist.

This canary twist wine glass is rare; the yellow twist is produced by colouring the glass mix with an oxide of iron or silver. The bowl is waisted and, typically of colour twists, has no engraving.

Mixed twists

Combinations of different types of twist are unusual and valuable. Some mixed air and opaque twist

stems were made, most of which are double series. The mixed coloured and air twist wine glass, *above*, is worth twice as much as

one with a standard coloured twist. The rarest and most valuable mixed twist includes all three types: an air, an opaque, and a coloured twist.

Composite stems

So many glasses with stems that included elements of all the popular stem types were made between 1745 and 1775, that they are described by a particular term: composite stems. These combine plain sections, balusters, twists and knops. Most include a plain section and an air twist with a knop.

This typical composite stem has an air twist above a beaded knop and a plain stem over a high conical foot. Opaque twists in combination are extremely rare.

Continental copies

Most colour twists are in fact Continental contemporary copies of English pieces, indeed, Dutch versions were produced in much larger quantities because there was no tax on coloured glass on the Continent, and these are worth only a tenth of English ones. They can be identified in a number of ways:

* Continental colour twists weigh less than their English counterparts and have no grey tint, as they are made from soda rather than lead glass.
* Their twists are inferior (see comparison pp.90–91).
* The threads lack the solidity in colour of English twists.
* They do not ring.

If in doubt always consult an expert as copies and contemporary versions abound.

FACET-STEMMED GLASSES

Facet stem wine glass with round funnel bowl, shoulder knop and flat foot c.1780; ht 6½ in (16cm); value code F

Identification checklist for 18thC facet stem glasses
1. Does the glass have a flat foot with no fold?
2. Is the foot wide and fluted?
3. Is the pontil mark ground out?
4. Is the stem section hexagonal?
5. Are the facets diamond, hexagonal or straight cut?
6. Is the stem elegantly proportioned and the glass well balanced?
7. Does the bowl feature any engraved, cut or moulded decoration?
8. If engraved, does the decoration include motifs such as vines, stars, flowers, birds and insects?

Facet stems
Facet stems date from 1775–1810 and represent the last of the distinctive 18thC stem forms. The mass production of cut glass was motivated by a combination of the Neo-Classical style of the late 18thC, illustrated by the architecture of the Adam brothers, and Josiah Wedgwood's pottery, and the additional excise tax on glass. The 1777 Act introduced duty on coloured glass, including

"enamel" glass, which meant that opaque twists became expensive to manufacture. Craftsmen were forced to develop alternative decorative techniques that served to reduce the weight of glass items.

Typical features
The development of grinding techniques in England and Ireland towards the end of the 18thC facilitated the production of faceted glasses, it also played a

part in altering many of the features which had remained constant for so long. Typical characteristics include:

* A round funnel bowl: older forms such as the trumpet and the bell could not be cut easily.
* A flat foot, which replaced the conical folded foot as the most common form.
* A ground-out pontil.
* Knops, such as the shoulder knop on the glass in the main picture, are unusual, and make facet stem glasses more valuable.

This facet stem glass was made for use on board ship, and pieces such as this one, with a short stem and a very wide foot – creating a low centre of gravity – are known as ship's glasses.

There are three main patterns of facet: diamond facets, seen on the glass in the main picture; hexagonal facets seen *above*; and flat-cut facets, see *above right*.

The stem section is usually hexagonal with six to eight bands of diamond or hexagonal facets, and sometimes stems also feature vertical flutes. Both facets and flutes can continue over the base of the bowl and appear as bridge flutes on the foot.

Decoration

The bowls of facet stems were sometimes cut with basal flutes, or featured moulded decoration such as honeycombing. Engraving was common and subjects include fruiting vines, stars, flowers, birds and insects. Some featured Jacobite symbols (see pp.96–97), such as the wine glass *below*, which has an extra row of facets on the bowl that appear as a rose when one looks into the glass.

* There are some extremely rare English facet glasses with Dutch political stipple engraving, which may have been made by or for Dutch exiles living in Britain.
* The value of a facet stem will depend on the complexity of the cut decoration on the stem and foot, and the subject of the bowl decoration.

Copies

The Stourbridge-based company Stevens & Williams (established 1856), made many facet-stemmed glasses around 1900. They can be easily confused with 18thC pieces, but the stems tend to be too thick and balance is therefore awkward. Engraving on later examples is also similar to that on earlier pieces, and subjects include flowers and birds and sometimes Chinoiserie.

JACOBITE AND WILLIAMITE GLASSES

Henry Brown Amen Glass
c.1740; ht 7⅜ in (18.7 cm); value code A

Identification checklist for early Jacobite drinking glasses
1. Does the glass have a drawn trumpet bowl?
2. Is the stem plain with a tear?
3. Is there a conical folded foot?
4. Are the size and proportions of the glass similar to other early 18thC drinking glasses?
5. Does the piece feature diamond-point engraving?
6. Is there a symbolic design?
7. If there is an engraved rose is there also a single bud?

Jacobite glasses
In the 18thC glasses were made in support of the bids by descendants of the Catholic James II and their sympathizers, to restore a more direct Stuart line in England. They were used for drinking loyal toasts which was an act of treason, and so owning one was a symbol of true allegiance.

Amen glasses
Glasses such as the one in the main picture are known as an "Amen" glasses because they feature verses from Jacobite anthems, ending in the word "Amen". This early Jacobite glass has a typical drawn trumpet bowl above a plain teared stem and a conical folded foot.

Jacobite symbolism

In addition to engraved anthems, Jacobite pieces also featured a variety of symbolic designs:
* daffodils and forget-me-nots which were mourning emblems;
* oak leaves derived from the Boscobel Oak, a tree in which Charles II is supposed to have hidden from the Parliamentarians, and is therefore a symbol of Stuart restoration;
* Latin phrases which became Jacobite slogans – for example, *Redeat* ("may he return");
* other symbols, including the royal crown, doves, thistles and butterflies.

The English rose was the most common emblem, and is believed to represent the English crown. This was often accompanied by one or two buds representing the claimants to the throne: James Edward Stewart, son of James II known as the Old Pretender, and his son, the Young Pretender or Bonnie Prince Charlie.

Another flower design was the lily-of-the-valley, a symbol of beauty, seen on this double series opaque twist cordial glass. It was

used because the Young Pretender was considered to be very handsome.

Fakes and copies
* Following a resurgence of interest in Jacobite engraved glasses at the end of the 19thC, many copies were made. These are larger than the originals and are relatively easy to identify.
* Some genuine 18thC glasses were engraved in the 1920s and 30s to enhance their value, these are very difficult to distinguish from the genuine article.

Value

All Jacobite glasses engraved during the 18thC are highly collectable, especially those made before 1745 while the Jacobite threat was still strong, and the possession of such pieces an act of treason. Glasses engraved with symbols only, such as roses, are described as being "of possible Jacobite significance", and are less valuable than those that can be positively attributed. Those produced after 1745 when ownership had been decriminalized are also worth less.

Williamite Glasses

Williamite glasses were made to commemorate the victory of William of Orange over James II at the Battle of the Boyne 1690.

This goblet c.1720, is dedicated to William and Mary and features engravings of the busts of the two monarchs. Other commemorative glasses show equestrian portraits and the date of the battle. They were specially made for, and collected by, the Irish market.

ENAMELLED AND BEILBY GLASS

A finely-painted opaque flared tumbler
c.1760; ht 4in (10cm); value code C

Identification checklist for 18thC Beilby drinking glasses
1. Does the glass have an opaque twist stem (other forms are less usual)?
2. Is the foot conical?
3. Is there opaque white enamelled decoration (coloured enamels are more unusual)?
4. Is the enamelling thinly applied and high quality?
5. Are there traces of gilding on the rim?
6. Is the piece in good condition?

Enamelled glass
Enamelling did not become a popular decorative technique in Britain until 1750. Enamel is made from powdered, coloured glass that is heated and then painted onto the glass surface. One group of enamelled glassware was made in Bilston in Staffordshire, in opaque white to imitate the white porcelain also made in the area. Items made in the Bilston area are functional – for example, cruets, candlesticks and tumblers such as the floral painted one in the main picture.

Beilby Glass
After 1760 when enamelling on glass became more common, two centres developed. The first was in Bristol, led by Michael Edkins who worked on coloured glass known as "Bristol" glass. The second, and most well known, was based in Newcastle led by the Beilby family.

The Beilby family of seven children began to produce enamelled glass, a technique developed by William, the fourth child, following the bankruptcy of their father's business. William had been an apprentice to an enamel maker in Bilston and during this time experimented with white enamels on clear glass. The family moved to Newcastle and started to produce pieces commercially, with William and Mary (the seventh child), the best known exponents.

enamel, and a needle was used for detail. Later, more ambitious designs include classical ruins, pastoral subjects, landscapes, as seen on the glass *below*, gardens and sporting scenes.

Royal and armorial Beilbys
The most valuable pieces are known as "Royal Beilbys", and were made to commemorate the birth of the Prince of Wales, later the Prince Regent, in 1762.

This example from around 1765 is typical: a wine glass with a double series opaque twist stem, conical foot, and detailed, enamelled sporting scene. There are also traces of gilding on the rim.

Identification
All Beilby glasses are valuable, but the glass *above* is more so because it is attributed to William himself. Very few pieces were personally signed, but detailed records were kept between 1767 and 1778.
* Beilby enamelling is found on glasses with other stem forms, including facet stems, and air and incised twists, but these are early examples and were probably made to special order.

Patterns and designs
Examples of early Beilby work feature simple decorative borders of flowers, fruiting vines, and hops and barley. These were made in thinly applied white

Other rare pieces include coloured armorial and commemorative pieces, often signed with the Beilby name.
* Armorial Beilbys are worth ten times more than ordinary ones.

RUMMERS

Sunderland Bridge rummer
c.1830; ht 8in (20cm); value code F

Identification checklist for late 18th and 19thC rummers
1. Is the glass sturdy with a short stem and a wide foot?
2. Is the mouth open and not turned in?
3. Does the glass have a capacity of 8–15fl oz?
4. Is the glass slightly grey in tone, and does the bowl ring when tapped?
5. Is the pontil rough, ground out, or tool marked (ie. not machine finished)?
6. Is the inside of the bowl free from scratches?
7. Is the base worn?

Rummers
For many years, "rummer", the word for a 19thC low drinking goblet, was thought to be a corruption of *roemer* (meaning "Roman-type"), a traditional German wine glass originally from the 15th and 16thC, with a flared foot and a stem with applied prunts. A few *roemers* were made in England at the end of the 17thC.

British rummers were used for drinking toddy (rum punch) or the naval drink, rum and water. They have a short stem, a wide bowl and a capacity of between 8 and 15fl oz (or 233–438ml).

Decoration
Made from around 1780, rummers were among the first English glasses to feature engraved decoration. The glass in the main picture was engraved to commemorate the opening of the Sunderland High Level Bridge. These glasses were made as souvenirs and the decoration is usually skilfully executed, and those that bought them could have initials engraved inside a cartouche on the reverse. Where this was carried out on the spot, the letters tend to be crudely finished compared with the rest of the decoration.

18thC Rummers

Georgian rummers date from 1780. Most were designed to be sturdy, hard-wearing tavern glasses, and featured only simple decoration – for example, a small amount of cutting on the body and foot. Sometimes feet were cut with stars, or made in the "lemon-squeezer" style (see pp.130–131).

* Rummers were usually made from lead crystal glass, although varying proportions of lead were used in the mix.

This elaborately-cut rummer is a high quality example of this type of glass, but it still has the characteristic wide mouth and short stem.

19thC Rummers

Heavy drinking glasses became popular again around 1820 and can be distinguished by the foot which is larger and thicker than Georgian rummers.

Simple cut patterns, such as diamond cutting see *above*, and engraved initials, names and plants are quite common, and from about 1810 rummers were engraved with hops and barley indicating that they were used for ale and beer. Shapes changed little as the practical nature of the glasses gave the glassmaker no incentive to experiment.

* Many rummers dating from the first half of the 19thC are scratched inside the bowl because drinks containing added sugar, such as toddy, were stirred using glass rods. While this is interesting, it is important to avoid damage when buying.

Coloured rummers

Coloured rummers are rare – 99 per cent were made in clear, crystal-type glass, although quality does vary enormously.

Some rummers were made in blue, such as this Bristol example from around 1800, and also in green and amethyst, but these are more unusual. They often had gilded decoration on the body, such as names, mottos, or simply gilding on the rim, as seen in this example. But because cold gilding was used, they are vulnerable to wear and few have survived in good condition.

Collecting

The relative inexpense and robust shape of rummers make them some of the most collectable and functional items of 18th and 19thC glass. They are highly sought after for table use.

* As rummers were heavily used their bases are invariably worn.
* Copies were made this century, but are quite easy to identify because the glass is too bright, and the feet are thin and machine-finished.
* Some sets of formal rummers exist: genuine sets of eight or more will command a premium.
* Check the quality of the metal: the glass should be heavy, have a grey tone and should ring.

18THC GLASS SHAPES

Knops

Knops, or decorative swellings found on the stems of drinking glasses, became a feature of 18thC English glassware. The discovery of lead glass, a softer and more malleable metal than Venetian *cristallo*, or northern European soda glass, facilitated the production of heavier, more elaborate stem forms. Lead glass cools more slowly than soda glass, is less brittle, and is therefore easier to manipulate.

Technique

Knops were produced by reheating a small section of a glass rod that was to become the stem of a glass, and then compressing this point until a knop was created. Some knops, such as the acorn and the mushroom were formed using shaping tools. Others including the bladed and the flattened knop were tooled.

Forms

The earliest knop form is the baluster, a shape derived from Renaissance architecture and popular in Britain around the beginning of the 18thC. There is the true baluster, where the widest part of the swelling is nearer the base of the stem, and the inverted baluster, with the widest part of the swelling towards the top.

Early 18thC drinking glasses became known as heavy balusters and are characterized by solid stems with large, well-defined knops in a variety of forms. Baluster (true and inverted), angular, and annulated knops are the most common. The acorn, bobbin, mushroom and cylinder knops are rare.

As glass forms became lighter, stems became more elongated and the knops less defined, such as those seen on light balusters and balustroids. Different types of knop appear in a huge number of combinations: the inverted baluster is the most commonly-found knop.

Knops are also found on glasses with air, opaque and colour twist stems, and composite, faceted and rudimentary stems.

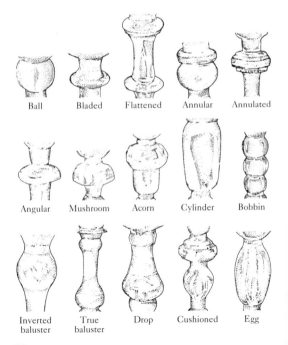

Ball   Bladed   Flattened   Annular   Annulated

Angular   Mushroom   Acorn   Cylinder   Bobbin

Inverted baluster   True baluster   Drop   Cushioned   Egg

Bowl shapes
The first 18thC drinking glasses, heavy balusters, had mainly pointed round funnel and conical bowls, while some were made with bell and thistle-shaped bowls. The drawn trumpet is particularly associated with the plain stem, while the ovoid bowl was found on many facet-stemmed glasses, and opaque twists often had round funnel or ogee bowls. However, there are a huge number of different combinations of bowl shape and stem form on 18thC drinking glasses.

The capacity of 18thC drinking glasses tends to be relatively small when compared to those made today: alcoholic drinks at the time were strong and were drunk only in small quantities.

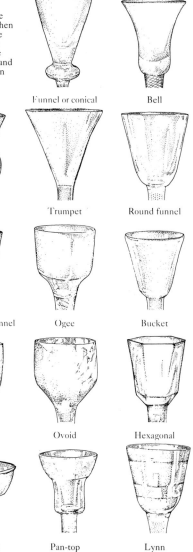

Funnel or conical

Bell

Thistle

Trumpet

Round funnel

Pointed round funnel

Ogee

Bucket

Cup

Ovoid

Hexagonal

Double ogee

Pan-top

Lynn

BRITISH AND IRISH DECANTERS

A rare, engraved English punch decanter, c.1770

Glass has been widely used to make vessels for storing, carrying and serving drinks for hundreds of years; glass serving bottles have come to be known as decanters. Strictly speaking, however, a decanter is used to hold a drink that has been decanted: poured from a storing vessel into a more decorative item, leaving behind a sediment, and ensuring that the liquid served at the table is clear. Decanters were originally intended specifically for wines with a sediment, such as port and Madeira, but the term now also describes bottles used to serve spirits (with no sediment), including whisky and gin.

The first glass bottles appeared in Britain in the 17thC. Previously serving vessels were made from leather, bone, metal and pottery. Squat, dark green bottles, with stamped glass seals date from around 1650. Seals were a sign of wealth and standing, and identified the owner, or the establishment to which the bottle belonged, and sometimes the date of manufacture. Seal bottles were originally free blown, but later examples (c.1730) were mould-blown or shaped with flattened sides so that they could be more easily stacked.

In the late 17thC, George Ravenscroft made a number of distinctively-shaped and ornamented jugs and decanters from his newly-developed "glass of lead", but decanters made in shapes that are familiar today were first made at the beginning of the 18thC. The "shaft and globe" form, with a long neck and a bulbous body extended throughout the 18th and 19thC, and formed the basis for many other decanter shapes. The mallet decanter began to emerge during the 1720s. This style had straight sides, sloping either slightly outward or inward, and varying lengths of neck. The slope of the shoulders then gradually increased and decanters were made taller; this shape became known as the shouldered decanter. Later 18thC forms include the bell (from c.1750), the taper (from c.1765), the barrel or Indian-club (c.1775), and the "Rodney" or ship's decanter (c.1780).

Early decanters tended to be plain, but the rising popularity of wheel cutting and engraving during the 18thC, together with the necessity of providing lighter glass items due to the 1745 Excise Act, meant that decorated decanters became more common. Ornamentation was not elaborate however, as this detracted from the appearance of the contents. Hexagonal faceting is often found on the necks and shoulders of decanters, with decorative cutting in the shape of festoons and stars on the body. Scale cutting, popular from c.1760, was used on shoulders and necks. Enamelling, most notably by William and Mary Beilby (see pp.98–99), is found on some 18thC decanters. Coloured decanters, originally made to hold spirits, were produced around the Bristol area from the 18thC onwards, mainly blue, but also green and amethyst.

In the late 18thC, decanters became more heavily ornamented with elaborate cut decoration, following the Anglo-Irish style (see pp.134–135). By the 19thC, decanters were made using many of the innovative techniques developed by British glasshouses and displayed at the international exhibitions held during this period, and shapes changed in response to the revivalist periods which characterized the Victorian era, such as the Neo-Classical style which was popular between c.1850 and 1880. The Arts and Crafts Movement of the late 19thC (see pp.120–121) favoured plain, simple forms for decanters, usually with a foot.

Most decanters, other than very early pieces or great rarities, are reasonably priced, and often cost no more than a good quality modern decanter, and have the added advantage of holding their value. Pairs of decanters are worth roughly three times the price of a single, and are desirable. And while larger sets of three or more are interesting, numbers will not dramatically increase the price. Always look for wear on the base of a decanter as a sign of authenticity – decanters are heavy, and if regularly used should be worn. Some wear is faked to give a false impression of age: if the base is looked at through a magnifying glass, faked wear will appear as a network of straight lines all running in the same direction, genuine wear is more irregular in appearance.

SEAL BOTTLES

A rare "shaft and globe" wine bottle
c.1660; ht 8in (20.5cm); value code B

Identification checklist for 17thC and early 18thC seal bottles
1. Does the bottle have a dark heavy glow, probably green under strong light?
2. Is the body free from seam lines?
3. Is the base rough with a kick?
4. Does the bottle have an unusual shape?
5. Is there a strong ring just below the top of the bottle?
6. Is there a seal on the side of the body?
7. If so, is there a date?
8. If a shaft and globe bottle, is the glass shiny?
9. If an onion bottle, is it in perfect condition?

Seal bottles
Around the middle of the 17thC, a group of dark green (almost black) bottles developed, and these probably represent the first items of specifically "British" glassware. The bottles were free-blown, and therefore have no seam lines, they are rough on the base (the site of the pontil), and they often have eccentric shapes. Used to serve wine, many of these early bottles are characterized by their "seal" which identified the owner when a bottle was sent back to the wine merchant to be refilled.

"Shaft and globe" bottles
The "shaft and globe" shape of the bottle in the main picture was one of the earliest forms: the oldest known seal bottle is dated 1657 and bears the seal of the King's Head, a tavern near Oxford. The strong ring around

the neck was used to tie a stopper onto the top of the bottle. The seal on the bottle in the main picture features an ox with the initials "R. B."; it has not been identified, but it was probably a tavern bottle. Seal bottles always have indentations or "kicks" in the base. The shaft and globe was common until c.1700.

* Seal bottles with dates are more desirable.

* Many seal bottles are found in water and therefore have a dull, water-damaged surface. Seal bottles that have been kept in good condition are shiny and are more valuable.

At the beginning of the 18thC, "onion" wine bottles, such as this one, became fashionable. Many of these also have seals, and a large number show the date of manufacture.

* Onion bottles are found sufficiently frequently for damage to affect value, and cracked or badly stained examples should be avoided. Small chips on the neck are acceptable, but damage to the seal will depress the price greatly.

* A shaft and globe with minor damage, such as the chipped rim on the bottle in the main picture, will be worth more than an onion bottle in perfect condition.

* Seals from broken bottles are collectable and inexpensive.

Low Countries or Britain?

Onion wine bottles are believed to have developed in the Low Countries and Britain at the same time. The seal on the example above suggests that it is British (it bears the name "T. Burford"), as no continental bottles with seals have been found. It can be difficult to identify the origin of plain bottles, but those from the Low

Countries are usually paler and have a lower kick in the base.

* It is important to be able to distinguish a Low Countries bottle from an English one: an English one may be worth up to four times more.

Manufacturers experimented with the shape of wine bottles during the first half of the 18thC; this was done mainly to aid storage, as the free blown onion shape did not lend itself easily to stacking. Shaped and moulded bottles were expensive to produce: some were marvered (rolled over a flat surface) to flatten and straighten the sides, but this very rare octagonal wine bottle has been blown inside a wooden shaper. The piece is dated 1738 and the seal bears the owner's name, "J. M. Reeves".

Late 18thC seal bottles

Towards the end of the 18thC, wine bottles began to be made in the form we know today: straight sides, sloping shoulders and a short neck. Made in green and dark brown glass, they were still free blown, and always have a kick in the base. Although corks and corkscrews were now being used, the strong ring was still present on the neck, and probably served to strengthen the bottle. A huge number of seal bottles exist, ranging from those belonging to aristocracy, local pubs, Oxford colleges and MPs. These may have been for use at Westminster or as electioneering gifts.

18THC DECANTERS

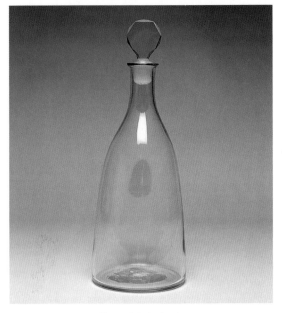

Magnum tapering decanter
c.1770; ht 14in (35cm); value code D

Identification checklist for mid-18thC decanters
1. Is there a kick in the base of the decanter?
2. Does the glass have a greyish tint?
3. Is the decanter relatively light in weight?
4. Does the decanter hold two imperial pints?
5. Is the stopper a variation of the lozenge or bull's eye design?
6. Is it in proportion to the bottle?
7. Is it a good fit but not airtight?
8. Does the texture of the stopper peg correspond with the texture of the inside of the neck of the decanter?
9. Where there is cutting or engraving, is it relatively restrained?

Late 17th–18thC decanters
Late 17thC decanters were made from heavy, mould-blown glass with high kicks in the base. Like seal bottles they were used for serving, and stoppers, where found, were loose corks or plugs secured with string. Between 1725 and 1730, a group of bottles called cruciform decanters were made. These were moulded with a large surface area for cooling.

Mid-18thC decanters
The magnum taper decanter in the main picture is an example of the earliest true decanter shape which began to appear in the mid-18thC. Made from lead crystal, the elegant form marks the transition from bottle to decanter, and glass stoppers instead of corks had begun to be used. They are usually left undecorated to display the colour of the wine,

although some are cut and engraved. Because of the excise tax levied on the weight of glass they were less heavy than their predecessors.
* The magnum is an usually large size: the usual capacity for an 18thC decanter is two imperial pints (a quart).

Decanter styles evolved rapidly in the second half of the 18thC, and new forms, such as this ovoid example with three applied neck rings, were produced.
* Neck rings evolved towards the end of the century both for decoration and to ensure that the vessel could be handled more easily and safely.

A rather rare form, this Indian club or barrel-shaped decanter features some restrained cutting characteristic of the period.
*Georgian decanters usually have

stoppers which are variations of the lozenge or bull's eye design – for example, plain or faceted. Stoppers acted as dust covers and were not designed to be airtight.

Where cutting occurred, it was limited to narrow fluting at the base and sometimes at the neck: this piece has a diamond-cut neck and faceted round stopper.
* The texture of the stopper peg should correspond with the texture of the inside of the neck of the decanter: they will be either ground or polished.

Engraving

Decoration remained simple throughout the period, although some were engraved, usually with floral or function-based motifs, such as fruiting vines. Some decoration was more elaborate, including cut and engraved festoons in the Neo-Classical style.

There is a group of shouldered decanters that have engraved labels, such as this port decanter *above*, which also features fruiting vines. Engraved labels exist for other fortified wines such as Madeira and claret.

Collecting

* Value is enhanced by size: larger decanters (with a capacity of more than two pints) are rarer and therefore more expensive.
* The rarity of the shape and decoration is another factor – for example, heavy cutting, and the subject on a label decanter.
* Sometimes the glass includes black and white flecks, caused by the mix being too hot or cold when the bottle was made. These are to be avoided.

REGENCY DECANTERS

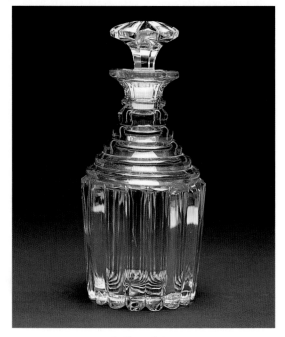

A pillar-cut decanter
c.1820; ht 11½ in (29cm); value code F

Identification checklist for Regency decanters

1. Does the decanter feel relatively heavy in weight?
2. Does it have a large body and a short neck?
3. Does the glass have a grey tone?
4. If there are rings on the neck, are they applied to the outside of the bottle?
5. Is there heavy-cut decoration?
6. Does the decoration include flutes and/or diamond cutting?
7. Does the decoration on the stopper match the decoration on the body of the decanter?
8. Is the decanter in good condition?

Regency decanters
The period of the Regency, 1811–1820, when George, Prince of Wales (later to be George IV) ruled on behalf of his father George III, was a time of great achievement in the decorative arts, and Regency styles were popular until c.1840. In the glass industry, 18thC gilded and engraved decoration was replaced by heavy cutting. Regency decanters, such as the heavy, pillar-cut example in the main picture, show clearly the extent of the glass cutter's skill.

Cut glass decanters
Initially the Regency style was based on horizontal bands or panels of deeply cut motifs such as relief or strawberry diamonds.

In around 1825 flat cutting in vertical flutes was introduced. The pillar-cut decanter in the main picture is a good example of opulent and stylish Regency decoration. Pillar cutting was the most expensive form of cutting, where the glass was cut into round flutes to imitate pillars; a large amount of glass had to be used in the production of the body to create this effect.

* Matched pairs can fetch up to three times as much as single decanters. Sets of more than four are very rare.

The neck rings and cut bull's eye stopper on this Regency decanter resemble those from the late 18thC. The cutting on the base and shoulders of the body, neck rings and the stopper, is unusually restrained for the period.

This barrel decanter shows all the characteristic decorative features of the Regency style: mushroom stopper, diamond cutting,

horizontal fluting and shallow body flutes. It also has a large body and short neck, which made decanters easy to handle.

Stoppers
The stoppers of Regency decanters are often cut and are usually variations of the mushroom stopper, although other shapes are found, such as the ball and bull's eye stopper.

Typical of the Regency period, this diamond-cut mushroom stopper features the same style of decoration (cutting or engraving) as the body of the decanter to which it belongs (see decanter *below left*).
* The quality of the cutting and the metal are important determinants of value.

Beware
* Condition is very important: look for scratches on the inside and chips on the shoulders and around the edge of the base. The glass should have a soft grey tone; brown or yellow tints which appear due to impurities in the mix should be avoided.
* Remember, a genuine Regency decanter should be worn on the base through use.
* There are a number of Continental copies of Regency decanters which usually have a brown tint, and which have non-British features such as heavily cut bases. They may also be lighter in weight than their British equivalent.
* Continental copies are worth only two-thirds as much as an original Regency decanter.
* There were revivals of the Regency style in the 1880s and 1930s. Often too bright in colour, they have neck rings that are moulded out of the body rather than applied, and are clumsy to handle. Those made in the 1930s have no status as collectables.

IRISH DECANTERS

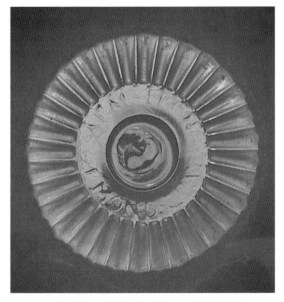

Detail of a marked base formed from a mould, Ireland c.1800; ht 3¾ in (9.5cm); value code C

Identification checklist for late 18th and early 19thC marked Irish decanters
1. Is the decanter full sized (two pint) with an ovoid form?
2. Are there moulded flutes on the base (cut fluting is less common)?
3. Does the decanter have a stopper with a moulded rim?
4. Is the rim slightly flared?
5. Is the stopper and neck polished out?
6. If engraved, are the subjects Irish, such as shamrocks and harps?

Irish decanters
The peak of Irish glass production (1760–1820) coincides with the development of the decanter. It is usually difficult to distinguish between English and Irish decanters made during this period, but a few Irish decanters are marked. This was done by blowing the glass into low moulds shaped like coasters, with the name of the manufacturer or retailer written inside. If the glass was blown deep into the mould, the name would appear on the base of the vessel.

Marked decanters
Coasters were intended to create uniformity in shape and were used to form decanters and rinsers; a base marked using a coaster is shown in the main picture. Unfortunately however, marks imprinted by the coaster were often obscured by cutting around the bottom of the decanter.
* The most common maker's name is the "Cork Glass Co.", but there are others including "Penrose, Waterford", "B. Edwards, Belfast", "Waterloo Co. Cork", "Francis Collins, Dublin".

The mark on the base shown in the main picture, "Armstrong Ormond Quay", is found only rarely. Decanters are never coloured and blue rinsers (seen here) are extremely uncommon.
* Some copies of decanters by the Cork Glass Co. were made this century; these are not engraved and have a bulge just above the fluting where they were pressed into the mould.

Unmarked decanters
Most Irish decanters do not feature identifiable marks, but display other characteristics which mean that the piece can be attributed to Ireland.

This decanter from around 1800 has a characteristically Irish form with a slightly ovoid body, moulded fluting on the base, milled neck rings and a stopper with a moulded rim. The stoppers are always polished in and frequently do not fit very well. Although unmarked, the double neck ring (where they appear, there are usually three) is typical of the Belfast area; the engraving, a rose, a shamrock and a thistle, commemorates the Act of Union of 1801.
* Another characteristic is the flared lip; any damage to this will detract from the value.

Size
All Irish decanters occur in full (two pint) or half (one pint) sizes, but marked examples seem only to be full size; there are no magnum decanters that can be positively attributed to Ireland.

This decanter is better quality than the one shown previously: instead of moulded fluting on the base, there is narrow-cut basal fluting, decorative wide flutes on the neck, and the mushroom stopper is ground in to fit well and create an air-tight seal.
* Some Continental decanters have moulded fluting on the base but these are never made from crystal, and usually have crudely-made, pressed spire or mushroom stoppers.

Another typical Irish style was all-over cutting, seen here on this decanter made between 1770 and 1790: the entire surface of the bottle has been shallowly cut. These pieces are rare and were expensive both to produce and buy. This particular form of cutting is found only on Indian Club (barrel-shaped) decanters, such as this one, or taper decanters.

CORDIAL AND PINT DECANTERS

A set of three cordial decanters in a lacquer stand
c.1800; ht 9in (23cm); value code E.

Identification checklist for 19thC cordial decanters
1. Is the stopper a small faceted ball (other types are more unusual)?
2. Are the neck and stopper ground out (later examples will be polished)?
3. Is the neck free from applied decoration such as neck rings (single rings are sometimes found)?
4. Is the decanter worn, especially on the base and around the shoulder of the bottle?
5. If there is a stand, does the bottle fit neatly into it?
6. If coloured, does the decanter have a gilded or enamelled label?

Cordial decanters
Cordial decanters, made towards the end of the 18th and the beginning of the 19thC, were made for sweet, alcoholic drinks, usually consumed in the mid-afternoon. The first examples, produced around 1780, were made in the Adam style (see p.94) decorated with engraved Neo-Classical draped festoons. Those made around the turn of the century featured more elaborate designs. Some cordial decanters were blown with separate compartments for different cordials, each with their own spout. These were usually clear in order to distinguish between the drinks, but some were coloured, with the names of the contents gilded or enamelled on the outside of the compartments.

Cordial decanters were often made as sets and presented in Sheffield plate, silver or lacquer stands, such as the one in the main picture. As each set is unique, it is very difficult to find bottles from other sets to fit particular stands. The bottle necks often had small rings to support the stoppers when in use.

This unusual barrel-shaped cordial decanter with a mushroom stopper, has a half-cut body which indicates that it was made to fit into a stand.
* Stoppers on cordial decanters are often small faceted balls which bear little or no relation to the decoration on the body.
* Because their necks are usually short, cordial decanters do not tend to have grip rings to facilitate more accurate pouring: this example has a single ring.

Pint decanters

Pint-sized decanters were made at the same time as all styles of early quart (two pint) decanters –

for example, the taper and the bell (see pp.126–127), and existed up until the early Victorian period, around 1850.

Around the turn of the 18th–19thC, some square, octagonal, cylindrical, oval, and hexagonal pint-sized decanters were made which had no larger counterparts. The hexagonal rum decanter *below left*, is a good example.
* Pint-sized decanters were made because in the 18th and early 19thC wine was served in pints.
* These unusual-shaped bottles were not free-blown, they were blown into moulds and decoration was added later.

* Some later square decanters however, had decoration that was introduced by the mould, such as the ribbed decoration on this Irish mould-blown decanter, and represent some of the first mass-produced glassware.

Decoration

Pint decanters are often cut but are rarely engraved. Bristol blue or green decanters were invariably made to hold spirits.

Value

* A pair of decanters may be worth up to three times as much as a single piece, because it is almost impossible to find a perfect match. Even if the stopper is missing from one of the bottles they may still be worth as much as two single decanters.
* Pint decanters are generally worth around half the value of full-sized ones and can be used today for storing/decanting port, or for individual wine servings.
* Cordials and pint decanters are good to collect: they are less expensive, and take up less room than their larger counterparts.

COLOURED DECANTERS

Magnum dark green Rodney decanter, engraved with fruiting vines c.1810; ht 12in (30cm); value code E.

Identification checklist for 19thC coloured decanters
1. If the decanter is a solid colour, is it blue or green (other colours are more unusual)?
2. If the decanter has a cork, is the neck free from grinding?
3. Does the decanter feel relatively heavy?
4. If more than one colour, are distinct layers of glass visible?
5. If cut, is the decoration elaborate?
6. Is there wear on the base?
7. Does it have a ground-out pontil?
8. If the stopper is coloured, does it match the body of the decanter?

19thC coloured decanters
Although not decanters in the strict sense, English coloured examples date from around 1810 and were made to hold spirits such as rum, brandy and Hollands (gin). The most usual colour for a decanter was blue, green was less common, and amethyst and amber were rare. Georgian coloured wine decanters are unusual as they do not enhance the appearance of the wine; when they do occur, however, they are heavy and elegant.

Rodney decanters
One of the most common of the early shapes for coloured decanters was the "Rodney",

designed by Admiral Lord Rodney for use on board ship. They are always a flattened onion shape – the basal width ensured stability – and are usually found in pint or quart sizes; larger examples such as the magnum Rodney in the main picture are rare. They are made to take cork stoppers, often with silver-plated mounts, and the inside of the neck is not ground out.

German-influenced coloured decanters

Prince Albert's influence led to an interest in German white wines, and a market for attractive serving bottles developed. Produced from around 1850, these decanters followed the tall, narrow shape of Hock wine bottles. First made in single colours, such as yellow, green and blue, they were soon decorated in multiple colours.

Common to much Victorian glassware, decoration was often elaborate: some bottles were richly cut, such as this red overlay decanter c.1865, others were made with multiple layers of different-coloured glass and gilded decoration. These pieces are rare and therefore quite valuable.

"Cased" or overlay bottles were made, where a clear glass bottle was overlaid with a layer of coloured glass and then either cut or engraved, as seen on the blue overlay Stourbridge bottle *above*, to give a decorative finish. These feel relatively heavy, and the different layers of glass are clearly visible.
* Flashed decanters with a very thin outer layer of glass were common on the Continent, especially in Bohemia. Engraved decoration on these bottles often features hunting and forest scenes. Fruiting vines are another common motif.

This decanter by F. & C. Osler is an unusual example of Victorian overlay decoration, with a characteristic bulrush pattern (see pp.156–157) cut into a green bottle cased with opaque white glass: white is usually found as a body colour. Lighter shades of green are created by deeper cutting.
* There are no deliberate fakes. Later decanters can be identified by acid polishing on the base, while older ones have a worn base and a ground-out pontil.

VICTORIAN DECANTERS

Early Victorian decanter
c.1840; ht 11in (28cm); value code G

Identification checklist for Victorian decanters
1. Is the decanter a shaft and globe shape (other forms are less common)?
2. Is the neck the same length as the body?
3. Does the decanter have a two-pint capacity?
4. Does the decoration on the stopper reflect the decoration on the body?
5. Is the decoration architectural in style?
6. If cut or engraved, does the design include motifs such as stars, ferns and fruiting vines?
7. If the stopper and the body are numbered, do they correspond?
8. Does the glass have a grey tone?
9. Is the decanter in perfect condition?

Victorian decanters
Victorian decanters dating from around 1840, were influenced by late Georgian and Regency styles, but were more elaborate. Their form was architectural with pointed stoppers and flamboyantly-shaped bodies. They often featured mixed styles of cutting and

bands of engraving. Some pieces have "Gothic" influences – for example, spandrels and arches with a strong vertical emphasis.

Shaft and globe decanters
The most common Victorian decanter was the shaft and globe, with a round fat body, and a neck

which is approximately of the same length. Most had a capacity of two imperial pints, although those made towards the end of the 19thC held the equivalent of a modern bottle (¾ of a litre).

Both the body and stopper of this early shaft and globe decanter from around 1850 are engraved with a fruiting vine, a popular design, and the long neck is scale cut. It also has a characteristic thick, applied neck ring.

The shape of this silver-mounted engraved claret jug by Richards & Brown, London c.1860, lends itself well to cutting and engraving: subjects often included stars or ferns. Other subjects are found, such as the fruiting vines seen here. Silver mounts will add to the value of a piece.
* Victorian decanters are relatively common so they need to be in mint condition to have any value.

This classic later Victorian shaft and globe decanter c.1880, is a style that is still copied today. It has a detailed cross-cut body and a matching stopper, but no grip ring: a clear break with the Georgian influence.

Stoppers
The stoppers of Victorian decanters usually reflect the decoration on the body. Some later shaft and globe decanters do have faceted ball stoppers which were supplied as less expensive alternatives by contemporary retailers. These decanters were made for serving wine, port and sherry.

Numbered decanters
Occasionally numbers appear on the stopper and the neck of the bottle, these should always correspond. Where a decanter and stopper appear to match, but the numbers are not the same, this suggests another decanter exists that would make up a pair.

Fakes and copies
Fakes have not been deliberately manufactured, but some later styles are still produced today and may be confused with older pieces. The colour of the body on early shaft and globe decanters will have a grey tone, but on later pieces the glass will appear almost as bright as on modern versions. Modern decanters appear to be white in colour and often have the name of the manufacturer acid-stamped on the base. If there is a manufacturer's mark, then it is almost certain that the item was made in the 20thC.

ARTS AND CRAFTS DECANTERS

An Arts and Crafts decanter
c.1880; ht 12in (30cm); value code F

Identification checklist for Arts and Crafts decanters
1. Does the decanter have a simple, thinly blown form?
2. Does it feel relatively light in weight?
3. Is the glass clear?
4. Has the clarity of the glass been emphasized, perhaps by the addition of a foot?
5. If there is decoration, has it been added by hand?
6. Does the decoration on the stopper match the decoration on the body?

The Arts and Crafts Movement
In the second half of the 19thC a group of artists, craftsmen and designers developed a new ideology for the decorative arts. It was based around two principles: a rebellion against mass-market, machine-made items, and an appreciation of the dignity and serenity of the Arts during the Middle Ages. Leading figures included the designer William Morris and the author and art critic John Ruskin.

Arts and Crafts glassware
John Ruskin took a particular interest in glass design. He described glass cutting as "barbarous", believed forms should emphasize the true beauty of glass, which he regarded as "its dulcility when heated and its transparency when cold". The decanter in the main picture illustrates Arts and Crafts principles, with a simple, clear, thinly-blown, functional form, and is light in feel and appearance.

The foot is another important feature: Christopher Dresser (1834–1904), an important Arts and Crafts designer and

spokesman championed the addition of feet to decanters "so that light may surround it as fully as possible" and enhance the look of both the glass and the wine. His book, *The Principles of Decorative Design* (1873) had a considerable influence on the decorative arts. * Decoration was restrained and carried out by hand "in front of the kiln".

The Arts and Crafts movement revived some older continental forms, such as this *kuttrolf* decanter. The shape, with a large surface area for cooling, was originally popular in Germany in the 16th and 17thC. *Kuttrolf* decanters were made in Britain between 1880 and 1914, and are often silver-mounted.

The Venetian influence
The Venetian style was also an influence on the new design ideology, especially when Venetian glassmaker Antonio Salviati opened a London showroom in 1868. British firms responded by producing Venetian-inspired pieces with applied decoration, ribbing, festooning and *filigrana*.

This jug from around 1870 has Venetian-style decoration including applied blue prunts and a ribbed, serpent-like handle.

James Powell & Sons (1835–1980)
One of the firms that worked most closely with the Arts and

Crafts movement was James Powell & Sons of Whitefriars, London. This silver and glass centrepiece, designed by Harry Powell in 1906, has a typical elegant and unconventional form.

LOCKING DECANTERS
AND TANTALUSES

A square crystal locking decanter with a patent locking mechanism
c.1895; ht 8½ in (21.5cm); value code F

Identification checklist for 19thC locking decanters
1. Is the mount silver (base metals are less valuable)?
2. Do the silver marks on the neck and the stopper of the bottle correspond?
3. Is the mount dated between 1890 and 1920?
4. Is the locking mechanism in perfect working order?
5. Is the key made from cut steel (silver was not used to make keys)?
6. Is there a patent mark (this makes a locking decanter more desirable)?
7. Is the bottle cylindrical or square-shaped (ie. with straight sides)?

Locking decanters
The locking decanter, dating from the late 19thC to around 1914, allows the contents to be locked away, and comprises an individual square decanter with a fitting on the lip, and sometimes also on the stopper.

Most fittings, such as the one in the main picture, were made in silver and are very desirable. Patent numbers and details marked on the fittings will make a piece more desirable.
* When buying, make sure the mechanism works perfectly, and that the silver is in good condition. Repairs involve removing the silver from the glass which is very expensive.

Tantaluses

Tantaluses were used during the 19thC and enabled the household supply of alcohol to be kept under lock and key. They usually comprise a stand, with a wooden or metal frame, holding three square or cylindrical spirit decanters (whisky, brandy, gin or rum). The box or stand has a locking bar or other fixture which secures the bottles in place (see *right*).

Features

Usually the bottles are made from cut glass, and frequently are not the highest quality – the value lies in the tantalus itself rather than the quality of the constituent parts. Stoppers are usually faceted balls. If cut decoration extends only part of the way down the body, this implies that part of the frame should fit where the cutting ends. The bottles should all match.
* Metal frames are usually made from silver plate, while solid silver examples are rare.
* Wooden frames are usually made from oak or mahogany and are occasionally mounted or inlaid with silver or silver plate.

Value

The value of a tantalus will be enhanced by a good quality, solid frame, good quality glass, and a complicated locking device that

is in perfect working order (if the key is missing they are often difficult to open). Additional features such as dates, dedications, connections with historical events, or sporting themes, can also increase value.
* Bottles are very difficult to replace, and new bottles, even if they fit in the stand perfectly, will reduce value dramatically.
* Patent marks for the locking mechanisms sometimes appear. One of the best known was registered by a man called Betjeman, an ancestor of the late John Betjeman, the Poet Laureate.

"Cave de Liqueur"

A French version of British tantalus, a "Cave de Liqueur" is a locking box usually decorated with high quality ornamentation, containing 4 decanters and 16 glasses (nearly always this number). The decanters can usually be lifted out to make serving easier. Unlike a tantalus they were made as a piece of furniture, and not as a portable item.

The bottles are invariably cylindrical or square, such as these *left*, and can be cut, engraved or gilded. The glasses should all match: square decanters and the feet of glasses in the same set are cut to match one another. This can also help to identify replacement glasses.
* Incomplete sets are much less desirable.
* Ornate boxes add to value.
* France is the best place to buy, particularly Paris.

WINE AND CLARET JUGS

*A Christopher Dresser claret jug by Hukin & Heath
c.1880; ht 11in (27.5cm); value code E.*

Identification checklist for silver-mounted wine jugs
1. Is the mount secure?
2. Does the glass body fit properly into the mount around the lip?
3. Is the plaster that fixes the mount to the glass free from marks and stains?
4. Does the hallmark on the lid match the one on the rest of the mount?
5. Is the glass free from damage?
6. Does the piece bear a manufacturer's mark?

Wine and claret jugs
Wine and claret jugs exist in silver from the mid-18thC and in glass from the end of the 18thC. Early jugs did not have a stopper or cover but can be distinguished from water jugs because they have a narrow, decanter-type neck. The Arts and Crafts claret jug in the main picture displays many features typical of this par-ticular style: the jug and the silver mounts have a simple form, and the plain glass body, free from engraved and cut decoration, enhances the colour of the wine. The low handle makes pouring easier, and the neck is wide, allowing the wine to breathe.

Dr Christopher Dresser (1834–1904)
Dr Christopher Dresser, a Scotsman, was originally a botanist but he became a silver and metalwork designer in the early 1860s. He designed the jug in the main picture in c.1875. Early examples of his work are always plain with silver or electro-plated mounts, but this style proved so popular that many vari-ations were produced. It was even made by Lindthorpe, the North Yorkshire pottery, in china.
* Dresser's designs are usually marked by the manufacturer, and Dresser is acknowledged as the designer on most pieces.

over Europe. The engraved fruiting vines indicate that the jug was made to hold wine.

Silver-mounted wine jugs
Silver-mounted jugs first appeared in c.1860. Most early examples are silver plated, but between 1880 and 1914 solid silver, hallmarked examples were quite common. Silver-mounted glass is highly sought after.

The most commonly-found claret jugs were made in the mid-19thC, such as this typical Victorian, Gothic-style piece from c.1840. It is identical to a decanter except that it has a pouring lip, a high, looped handle, and a stopper that is taller than the highest point of the handle. Nearly all Georgian and early Victorian claret jugs have high handles which makes accurate pouring very difficult.

Coloured wine jugs
A number of coloured jugs were made during this period. Not made to hold claret, they were used to serve white wines or champagne, or were simply decorative pieces. They were often given as wedding gifts.

This silver-mounted wine jug was made by the Stourbridge firm Stevens & Williams, and is dated 1889. It is typical of later Victorian fancy decoration found on decanters. The colour of the glass is not ideal for red wine, and may have been used to serve white. The handle is set quite low down to facilitate pouring.

Collecting
* Before buying, check that the plaster holding the mount onto the glass is secure, because washing can cause this to come loose. Once the glass falls out of the mount, the jug is ruined.
* If the plaster is stained and dark it may need replacing.
* If the mounts are hallmarked, check the date: silver-mounted glass jugs are still being made.
* If hallmarked, check that the date on the lid matches the mount as they are often replaced.
* Check for damage under the silver because the glass around this area is very vulnerable.
* Ornate silver mounts will increase the value of a piece.
* Check that the glass body fits snugly into the mount around the pouring lip, if it does not then it could be a replacement.

The cranberry wine jug *above*, made in around 1869 was manufactured in Stourbridge, but similar pieces were produced all

DECANTER SHAPES

Georgian stoppers
The stoppers on Georgian decanters are always variations on the lozenge (see *top left* and *top centre* (a faceted lozenge)) and the bull's eye (see *top right* and *bottom left* (an Irish moulded bull's eye)). These styles are all from the 18thC.

The mushroom stopper (see *bottom centre*) is from c.1800, and the later mushroom stopper, c.1830, (see *bottom right*) is cut with flat panels.

Ravenscroft jug
1680

Shaft and globe seal bottle 1680

Cruciform decanter
c.1725

Bell-shaped decanter
c.1770

Taper decanter
c.1770

Ovoid decanter
c.1780

Prussian decanter
c.1800–1810

Ship's decanter
c.1820

Georgian claret jug
c.1820

William IV decanter
c.1835

Mid-Victorian shaft
' and globe c.1850

Victorian claret jug
c.1880

Arts and Crafts
decanter c.1870

Coloured wine
decanter c.1870

Victorian stoppers
The stoppers of
Victorian decanters
usually reflect the
decoration the body
of the bottle, with the
same style of cutting
or engraving. Some
later shaft and globe
decanters have
faceted ball stoppers,
that were offered as
less expensive alter-
natives by glass retail-
ers during the period.
Sometimes a
stopper will be num-
bered, and therefore
the bottle of the
decanter should be
marked with the same
number.

ENGLISH AND IRISH CUT GLASS

An Anglo-Irish, step-cut, crystal jug, c.1830

Cutting as a decorative technique began in the 1stC BC and many examples of Roman and Early Islamic cut glass exist. The skills seem to have been lost around the 10thC, and cutting was not used widely until the beginning of the 17thC in Bohemia. Methods developed rapidly and the production of cut glass spread across Europe.

According to contemporary documentation cut glass first appeared in Britain at the end of the 17thC, but no examples have survived and advertisements from newspapers and journals of the time suggest that the majority of cut glass found in Britain during the first 20 years of the 18thC was imported. For example, the *London Gazette* from 1 October 1709 informed the city, "there is lately brought over a great parcel of very fine German cut and carved glasses, viz jellies, wine and water tumblers, beer and wine glasses with covers and divers other sorts. The like hath not been exposed to public sale before". But ten years later an advertisement placed by a glass cutter called John Akerman, in the *Whitehall Evening Post* implies that the cut glass he was selling was home-produced. By the early 18thC, British lead crystal had been developed which was softer and less brittle than its Continental counterpart, and was better suited to the cutting process. Akerman subsequently rose to hold the mastership of the Glass Sellers' Company (the controlling body of glassmaking and retailing) between 1740 and 1748, and was the first glass cutter to do so. It is known that Akerman employed at least one German cutter, possibly as a teacher to his English apprentices.

The development of cut glass in England was hampered by the 1745 Excise Act which encouraged the production of thinner glass that was less well suited to cutting; the Act did not apply to Ireland, and a thriving glass industry became established there. Cut glass was produced by Irish and English craftsmen in Ireland in the late 18th and early 19thC, and a style of glass developed known as Anglo-Irish.

Cut glass was, however, produced by all major English manufacturers in the 1820s and 30s, including W. H., B. & J. Richardson, Thomas Webb & Sons and Apsley Pellatt. Broad, flute-cut Regency-style glass was popular at this time, and contemporary pattern books from all these firms feature items with this type of decoration. After 1840 diamond cutting was reintroduced, and by the time of the Great Exhibition of 1851 (see pp.156–157), following the repeal of the Excise Tax on glass in 1845, highly elaborate cut designs were being produced reflecting a new era of industrial prosperity. F. & C. Osler were the leaders in this field in terms of the quality of their pieces.

There are four main processes involved in cutting. First the piece is marked: the required pattern is drawn onto the blank glass body, originally using a mixture of red lead and turpentine, now a permanent black felt-tip pen. Second, the item is roughed: the main lines of the pattern are cut into the glass using a power-driven (first by the feet or water, then steam, now electric) iron wheel which has a steady stream of fine wet sand running over it to act as an abrasive on the surface of the glass. The wheel is either flat, curved, or "v"-shaped, depending on the shape of the cut required. Roughing does not cover the whole of the pattern, and the cuts are coarse and dull with an unattractive appearance. The third and possibly most important process involves smoothing the glass using a variety of sandstone wheels, with a continuous flow of water running over the cutting surface for cooling and for lubrication. The wheels have a similar-shaped cutting edge to those used in the roughing process, but many different-sized wheels are used to cut the detail of the pattern onto the glass, with the smaller lines being cut exclusively at this stage, without previous roughing. The accuracy of the cutting relies solely on the skill of the crafts-man: one of the most obvious signs of poorly-cut glass is small inaccuracies, particularly on the base, where all the points may not meet precisely in the centre. The final, and traditionally the most time-consuming process, is polishing: here a wooden wheel with a fine abrasive surface is worked over all the cut lines, and is often finished with a felt wheel.

Polishing gives a final shine to the piece. From the begin-ning of the 20thC polishing has usually been carried out by acid-dipping, using a mixture of hydrofluoric and sulphuric acid which removes a minute layer of glass from the surface and leaves a very bright finish. However, the uniformity of the surface, with no wheelmarks, can have a flat, bland appearance, which also lacks some of the sharpness of hand-finished glass.

IRISH CUT-GLASS BOWLS

Irish cut-glass oval bowl
c.1810; ht 9⅝ in (24.5cm); value code D

Identification checklist for late 18thC and early 19thC Irish cut-glass bowls
1. Are there two or more different types of cutting (single styles are more unusual)?
2. Is the stem short and sturdy?
3. Is the foot a square-cut "lemon-squeezer" shape (other forms are less usual)?
4. Does the bowl have a slightly irregular shape?
5. Does the glass have a pale grey tone?
6. Does the design appear regular and complete?
7. If there is a "lemon-squeezer" foot, are the edges smooth?

Irish bowls
Bowls represent one of the typical luxury cut-glass items produced in Ireland between 1780 and 1835, and unlike some British-made cut glass, many bowl forms can be clearly attributed to the Irish glass-making industry. Three main shapes developed towards the end of the 18thC: the canoe or boat shape, the kettledrum, and the turn-over rim.

Bowls were made mainly as decorative pieces for the dining table, and were more usually filled with a display, often flowers, than used for serving food.

Boat-shaped bowls
The shallow diamond-cut bowl in the main picture is a high-quality example of Irish craftsmanship. The cutting on this bowl is relatively modest, but it has a typically ornate rim. There are a variety of stem types, but they are usually short and sturdy. The most common form of foot is the square-cut "lemon-squeezer" shape, which was moulded separately with ribbing impressed into the underside, and attached to the bowl before cutting. The foot is not always set parallel to the longest side of the bowl, sometimes it is joined at an angle.

This type of foot was also found on tableware such as covered jars and salt cellars as well as some drinking glasses.

The Kettledrum
Kettledrum bowls were often larger than other forms, and commonly featured bands of two or more different types of cutting.

This bowl, from the early 19thC, features scale cutting on the body, diamond cutting on the lip, and notched cutting on the rim. Sometimes the rims were left uncut. Kettledrum stems are usually short and sturdy, occasionally with a simple knop, and the feet are plain and round: lemon-squeezer feet are rare.

The turn-over rim
Bowls with a turn-over rim were the most difficult to manufacture and the most expensive. Once again cutting appears in bands of two or more different types, which usually extends to the edge of the rim but is less ornate than the decoration on canoe-shaped bowls. Turnover rims always have lemon-squeezer feet.

Typical of many Irish pieces, this bowl with two different forms of scale cutting is slightly lop-sided, and common to most Irish crystal produced in this period, the metal is slightly grey in colour

(more so than the usual lead crystal tone), possibly due to impurities in the mix.

The early, plain bowl *below*, from around 1780 has a lemon-squeezer foot with edges cut with grooves to disguise damage: this type of foot was always finished with a smooth edge, and any variation, such as rounding-off or cutting, suggests restoration work has been carried out. Lemon-squeezer feet should not be confused with plain cut square feet.

* The bobbin stem on this bowl is very rare; an unusual stem form will increase the value of a piece.

Collecting
* Bowls that measure more than 11in (28cm) high and 15in (38cm) long will be worth slightly more than smaller examples.
* The functional nature of bowls means that they are often scratched; those that are least scratched are the most desirable.
* Bowls should always have wear on the base.
* Some cut glass bowls were made without feet. These are relatively inexpensive and can be a good area in which to collect.

Repairs and restoration
* Many Irish bowls have been re-cut to disguise chips and other damage to the rims and feet: look for irregularities or incompleteness in the design. Re-shaping will be obvious to an expert so always seek advice.
* If a piece needs to be restored discuss the desired shape with a dealer before any work is done. If the damage is not too great then it is best not to alter the shape.

Copies
Copies of Irish bowls are not known, but these forms have been made ever since. Modern versions are very bright in tone.

CUT-GLASS SERVING PIECES

A pair of cut glass jars and covers, possibly Irish
c.1800; ht 13⅜ in (34cm); value code D

Identification checklist for 18thC and early 19thC Irish cut-glass jars
1. Is the piece well-balanced and well-designed?
2. Does it have a square foot (other styles are less usual)?
3. Does it have a high domed cover with a well-cut finial?
4. Are the body and the cover cut with the same pattern?
5. Are the foot and the rim smooth, regular and free from recutting?
6. Is the glass slightly grey in tone?
7. Does the piece feel relatively heavy?

Serving pieces
Cut-glass serving pieces other than bowls were also produced by craftsmen in Ireland between 1780 and 1840. A wide range of pieces are available including covered jars, sweetmeat glasses, butter dishes, salt cellars, vases, plates, jugs and wine coolers.

Typical features
The pair of jars in the main picture are a good example of high-quality cutting. Designed for display as purely decorative items, they exhibit many features typical of serving pieces from this period: a square-cut foot, a high-domed cover, and an ornately-cut finial.
* Jars were usually made in pairs and sometimes in sets of three. Single jars are collectable, but will be worth only a third or a quarter of the value of a pair.
* These pieces have been

widely copied. Original items should be well-balanced, no larger than 15¾in (40cm), and the glass should have a slightly grey tone. Continental copies tend to be over-sized, and the glass is either very grey or clear, with the characteristic tone of Irish glass.
* Look out for re-cutting and replacement lids; the decoration on the cover should echo the design on the main body.
* Some cut glass items appear in contemporary manufacturer's pattern books, and this can help to identify pieces. But in general it is still quite difficult to determine the origin of individual wares.

cutting. A genuine butter dish will have a stand, all the elements will have the same tone and the same form of cutting. They never have feet or cut-outs in the lid for a butter knife: if one is present it will be due to damage.
* A butter dish with all its elements complete will be worth much more than one with a piece missing.
* Coolers are not to be confused with preserve jars which do have feet and a cut-out for a spoon.

Silver-mounted glass
Silver-mounted glass is interesting to the collector because it can be dated accurately. It is important to check, however, that the silver decoration has not been added to disguise damage and that the mount fits securely.

This sweetmeat glass from around 1750 has a combination of features generally found on pieces made either before or after this date: a domed foot, faceted stem and large bowl. The cut-glass lip shows that it is not a drinking glass.

This silver-mounted pounce pot is hallmarked London, 1798. It was most probably ordered from an Irish glasshouse by a London retailer, and finished on arrival. Pounce was fine sand used instead of blotting paper.

Copies
Some styles of Irish cut glass have proved so popular that they have been copied ever since.
* Square feet on later examples are often thin and insubstantial.
* Late 19th and 20thC copies feature acid polishing which indicates a non-Irish origin.
* More recent ones should be relatively easy to detect because they lack the elegance of period examples, and the tone of the glass is often too bright.

One of the most collectable pieces of Irish cut glass is the butter dish or cooler. This is a typical example with straight sides, a domed lid and intricate

ANGLO-IRISH CUT GLASS

Anglo-Irish cut glass jug
c.1840; ht 11in (28cm); value code F

Identification checklist for Anglo-Irish glass, c.1830–1850
1. **Does the piece feel relatively heavy and appear slightly grey in tone?**
2. **Does it have an elegant form?**
3. **Is the piece well-balanced and in proportion?**
4. **Is the cutting high-quality but restrained?**
5. **Is there a single style of cutting?**
6. **Is the piece free from gilding or enamelling?**
7. **If engraved, is there a simple panel?**

Anglo-Irish cut glass
Taxation on glass in England forced many craftsmen and glass-making companies to transfer production to Ireland in the late 18th and early 19thC. As a result a style known as "Anglo-Irish" developed, which combined elegant English forms with high-quality Irish craftsmanship. When similar restrictions were imposed in Ireland, many people returned to England, but this type of glassware continued to be made in both countries until around the time of the Great Exhibition.

English or Irish?
The wine jug in the main picture shows typical Irish-style pillar cutting on the body, a step-cut neck, and a high looping handle, but the elongated shape suggests that it was probably made in an English factory.
* British cut glass made around 1840 is difficult to attribute positively: the jug could have been made either in England or Ireland, although the more fashionable shape of this piece implies that it was produced in England, following the popular

forms of silver vessels of the day.
* Anglo-Irish pieces tend to be made from good crystal glass and will therefore feel relatively heavy and are slightly grey in tone; later pieces will appear brighter.
* Anglo-Irish cut glass never features additional decoration, such as gilding or enamelling. Engraving appears occasionally, usually as a simple panel with a crest, initials, or a coat of arms.

This celery vase also illustrates a typical combination of features. The bands of different styles of cutting and the bladed knop are characteristic of Irish pieces from the 1830s, but the slight flare in the bowl, making the vase less sturdy and more elongated and elegant, was also found on English china vases from the 1840s.

This butter dish and stand c.1840, demonstrates the technical quality of Irish cutting, but it has an English form and a single style of cutting (strawberry diamonds) on all three elements, which is also typically English.
* The date of manufacture means that this piece is classified as

"Victorian", but the restrained nature of the cutting is not typical of Victorian over-ornamentation which appeared after 1840, and has more in common with Regency styles of cut glass.

The decoration on this preserve jar has a more characteristic Victorian style. The sturdy shape and technical quality are Irish in origin, but the flamboyant cutting is comprised of only one style of cutting. The rim appears to have been recut to disguise a chip, and the finial on the cover seems over-large and too long, and it may therefore, have been produced accidentally.

Collecting
The fact that a piece can be called Anglo-Irish will give it no added value; such items are interesting because they exhibit a transitional style that existed due to political circumstances. While the quality of most Anglo-Irish cut glass is very high, the attractiveness of individual wares is variable, and collecting becomes a matter of personal taste.
* Other wares include dishes, bowls and centrepieces. Smaller pieces are not so common because they did not lend themselves so well to deep cutting and intricate decoration.
* The prices of 19thC Anglo-Irish wares compare favourably with similar items of comparable quality made today and will hold their value over time.
* Later versions of Anglo-Irish styles have been made, but have brighter metal, will not feature characteristic irregularities in shape, and will not be worn.

MISCELLANEOUS 19THC CUT GLASS

Large Irish cut-glass plate
c.1820; dia. 9in (23cm); value code G

Identification checklist for 19thC cut glass plates
1. Is the piece approximately the size of a dessert plate (8–9in (20–23cm) in diameter)?
2. Does the plate have a large, flat centre with a flat, low edge?
3. Is the plate good-quality with a heavy metal body?
4. If there is cut or engraved decoration, is it on the underside of the plate?
5. Is there no kick on the underside?
6. Does the piece have an edge that is relatively plain (Continental examples are often cut)?

19thC glass plates
Glass plates are an unusual and relatively inexpensive item, made throughout the 19thC. The rare Regency example in the main picture is a good example. They are usually the size of a china dessert plate (8–9in (20–23cm) in diameter), with a flat centre section and a low, flat edge. The quality and extent of the cutting on this piece is exceptional; cut decoration often includes only a star under the centre of the plate, and some detail on the rim. Continental glass plates tend to have more ornate decoration on the rim. Glass plates of this size are rare because they were difficult and costly to produce: they were spun in a way similar to the production of window glass (see pp.150–151), and not pressed. They were made in small numbers throughout the 19thC and can be found in clear, coloured and overlay glass, and with engraved and etched decoration.
* Glass plates can be distinguished from glass stands because there is no kick in the base.

* Sets of six or more will be worth a good deal more than six times the value of one plate.

Caddy bowls

The importance attached to tea drinking in Britain in the 18th and 19thC led to the production of some expensive glass accessories. Tea was often kept in a tea caddy, a box made from wood, silver or ivory, and towards the end of the 18thC a compartment was added to hold a glass bowl for serving sugar.

Caddy bowls, such as this Bristol example c.1810, have a very distinctive shape which never varied, with tall sides and a small rudimentary foot. Coloured bowls (seen here) were made for lacquer caddies, but caddy bowls are usually clear with cut or engraved decoration. Pressed bowls were made from the mid-19thC.

Bulb vases

Vases made to support sprouting bulbs are very common items. The bodies were designed to disguise the roots of the bulb as they grew downwards.

Produced from the 18thC onwards, bulb vases can be found in a variety of forms including cut as well as coloured glass.

The left-hand vase in the picture *below left*, is typical of those from first half of the 19thC, with a narrow saucer or lip, a high kick in the base and a roughly broken pontil. Later Victorian examples, such as the vase on the right, have wider saucers and more unusual forms: this squat shape was reasonably common.
* Colours include blue, green, amethyst, brown and amber; red is the most unusual.
* Some bulb vases have factory and patent marks which make them easy to date.
* While early bulb vases are desirable, decorative quality is the most important determinant of price. Simple, common early 19thC vases will not be as valuable as rare late 19thC examples.

Obelisks

Glass obelisks were made in all lead crystal-manufacturing areas from the mid-19thC onwards. They were cast from a block of glass and then cut into shape. Perfectly transparent blocks of glass were difficult to achieve, and therefore obelisks were not easy to produce.

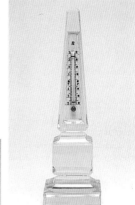

Some obelisks were fitted with thermometers attached to a vitreous plaque (see *above*), while others were enamelled on one or two out of (usually) three sides, giving an unusual visual effect.
* Check that the plaque fits well: if it does not, then it could be a replacement.
* Modern examples are made but are rarely set on a plinth.

GLASS LIGHTING

A George IV chandelier, c.1820

Glass lighting has been produced for centuries; the most notable early examples are probably glass shades for a group of mosque lamps made in the Middle East in the 12th–14thC (see pp.72–73). A number of these lamps still exist in private and museum collections, and were copied by the French Art Nouveau glassmakers at the end of the 19thC. The commercial production of glass lighting started in the late 17thC following the development of lead crystal, and had begun to flourish by the end of the 18thC.

Up until the end of the 19thC candles provided the main source of artificial light, and candlesticks were made in a number of materials, ranging from wood to precious metal set with jewels. Lead crystal glass provided the ideal medium for candlesticks because of its reflective qualities, and it could be made thick and clear, or heavily cut. They were usually made in pairs in order to magnify the production of light by reflecting off one another. The shapes of candlesticks broadly followed the fashions of the stems of 18thC drinking glasses (see pp.78–79), but were also influenced by styles of furniture. Candlesticks were expensive, luxury items, and therefore the Excise Tax of 1745 had less of an impact on their overall cost.

Multi-branched candlesticks, or candelabra, developed from the candlestick. These too were luxury items that tended to be used in the main rooms of large houses. They were extremely fragile with many delicate parts.

The reflective qualities of cut glass were utilized further by the development of lustres, which were cut-glass prisms attached around the candle or other source of light. The edges of the drip pan or sconce would be pierced, and long, cut-glass drops would be hung from it. The drip pan, an applied glass ring, was placed over the candle holder and prevented wax from dripping down the candlestick. These were made in sets of two or more to maximize the production of light. Towards the end of the 19thC these decorated candlesticks, which came to be known as "lustres", were manufactured in characteristically ornate Victorian styles: coloured, painted and gilded examples were made, principally as decorative items because they did not reflect light as effectively as clear glass pieces.

Chandeliers are not the most efficient form of glass lighting, but are the most impressive. The production of chandeliers is highly skilled and the work is extremely intricate: a medium-sized chandelier usually has several thousand parts. Originally intended to hold candles, chandeliers were modified to use gas after the 1830s, when metal gas pipes were incorporated into the branches. They are now powered by electricity and glass arms have been reintroduced. Glass is often combined with other media, such as ormolu, pottery and even silver. Architects such as Robert Adam and Vanbrugh designed large numbers of chandeliers. Many were designed for particular rooms, and should therefore be regarded as an architectural as well as a decorative feature. Large chandeliers are very expensive to maintain and are most often seen in public buildings and stately homes.

Glass has also been used as covers or shades for lamps, to protect the source of light from draughts, wind and rain, and was especially important for lights used outside. Glass was not usually used to cover a flame entirely, because direct heat tended to cause the glass to crack, instead glass covers protected the sides of the flame. When glass covers were used they were fixed well above the heat. Shades for candles – glass tubes which fit around the flame – were also made in Britain and can still be found in India, the West Indies and the Far East.

Glass lighting is a relatively expensive area of antique glass collecting. It is important to remember that items such as chandeliers and wall lights, are often sold by furniture dealers and at furniture auctions rather than by specialist glass dealers or at glass sales. Pairs of candlesticks, lustres and wall lights are worth three to four times the price of a single piece; this does not apply to most central lights or chandeliers, but pairs of hall lanterns are desirable.

18THC CANDLESTICKS

*A colour twist candlestick
c.1765; ht 8¼ in (20.5cm); value code B*

Identification checklist for 18thC candlesticks made before 1770
1. Does the candlestick have a popular 18thC stem form?
2. Is it made from high-quality lead crystal?
3. Does the candlestick feel relatively heavy?
4. Is the foot wide, heavy and possibly domed and terraced?
5. Is the stem knopped?
6. Does the candlestick measure 8–10in (20.3–25.4cm) in height?
7. Is it in good condition?
8. If the candlestick is straight and sconced, is there a (removable) pan to collect the wax?

18thC candlesticks
In the 18thC glass candlesticks were relatively uncommon, and silver, being less expensive, was a more widely-used material. Made from around 1730, they were high quality, luxury items, and tended to be made with the same forms as the stems of 18thC drinking glasses. Air twists were made between 1750 and 1760, opaque and colour twists between 1760 and 1775. The double-series colour-twist candlestick in the main picture is a good example. This one is particularly unusual because blue twists were very rarely found in candlesticks. The domed and terraced foot added stability to the candlestick, but also increased its weight, making it subject to a high level of tax.

This moulded pedestal or Silesian-stemmed candlestick from around 1745 differs from contemporary drinking glasses because the stem is heavier at the bottom making the candlestick more stable. It also has a heavy, domed and terraced foot.
* All 18thC glass candlesticks are 10–20 times more rare than drinking glasses with similar stem forms. However they are only two or three times more expensive, making them an interesting area in which to collect and invest.

Facet-stem candlesticks
One candlestick stem form that was not made only at the same time as its drinking glass equivalent is the facet stem.

More common than other forms, the facet stem was made between 1740 and 1880 and pieces are quite difficult to date accurately.

But the example *below left*, was made c.1770: it has a domed foot, rarely found on glassware made after this date.
* This piece has a removable sconce; these fittings are often lost but if present then the value of the candlestick is enhanced.

Taper candlesticks
Taper candlesticks, are identical in form to other 18thC candlesticks but are very small, usually no more than 4in (10cm) high (candlesticks usually measure 8–10in (20.3–25.4cm) in height), and have very fine stems.

Also known as tea candlesticks (as it is possible that they were used at the tea table), taper sticks were made to hold a taper used to light the household candles, and to supply a flame for melting sealing wax. A taper candle was about the size of a pencil.
* Taper sticks are usually produced singly, unlike full-sized candlesticks which were generally made in pairs.

Collecting
* Be wary of later facet-cut candlesticks which can be deceptive: they are often not made from crystal and are over-shaped.
* Copies were made in Holland in the 19thC, and in Britain in the early 20thC. The recent, British-made candlesticks are taller and larger than might be expected. These are made from lead crystal and are heavy, but Dutch copies were made from soda glass and therefore weigh much less.
* Pairs of candlesticks will be worth four times the value of singles (apart from tapers).
* Examine a piece carefully for damage: cracks caused by heat are quite common.

CANDELABRA AND LUSTRES

A George III glass candelabra (one of a pair)
c.1800; ht 22in (56cm); value code (for a pair) C

Identification checklist for late 18th to late 19thC candelabra
1. Is the candelabra made from a mixture of materials?
2. Do all the glass pieces match (for example, colour and style of cutting)?
3. Is the candelabra well-proportioned?
4. Is there a glass bead at the top of each drop?
5. Are all the drops in place?
6. Is there a finial at the top (such as a crescent or a pineapple)?
7. Is the candelabra easy to dismantle?

18thC candelabra
"Candelabra" is a relatively modern word. Throughout the 18thC the terms lustre, branches and girandoles (meaning "cluster") were used interchangeably to describe all kinds of glass lighting – ranging from a candlestick to a hanging chandelier. But by the end of the 18thC, "candelabra"

came to mean a multi-armed candlestick. The earliest examples of candelabra date from about 1750.

Features
The arms of candelabra usually slotted into a brass plate at the top of the base and could simply be lifted out for cleaning. The example in the main picture has a pineapple finial (a symbol of welcome), but more commonly the finial was a crescent – a style made popular by the fashion for *à la Turque* (in the Turkish style) at the end of the 18thC.

Victorian candelabra
The Victorian tendency for over-decoration also affected candelabra, and highly-ornate, and coloured pieces were produced.

This heavily-decorated example from the mid-19thC is high-quality, but the coloured glass and brass tooling do not maximize the production of light.
* Clear glass candelabra are more collectable than coloured pieces.
* A pair is worth four times as much as a single candelabra.

Condition
* Check that all the drops are present – replacing them can be expensive.
* Redundant holes in the base of the candelabra suggest that something has been altered or is missing. There are usually an even number of arms so the piece should look balanced.

Lustres
The term "lustre" is used to describe a candlestick with a drip pan from which rods of faceted

glass are suspended to catch and enhance the light. In fact "lustres" themselves are the glass drops hanging from the drip pans.

The candlesticks to which lustres were attached were often not made from glass – the bases of the Regency lustres *above* are made from gilt bronze. The long, flat cuts on these lustres will maximize the production of light, and the small beads help the lustres to hang more easily and allow some movement, adding to the overall effect.

During the Victorian period lustres also became bigger and more colourful, with larger and more complicated drops, such as those on this green and white overlay lustre from c.1880. Generally made in pairs, they were intended to catch and reflect the light.

CHANDELIERS AND LANTERNS

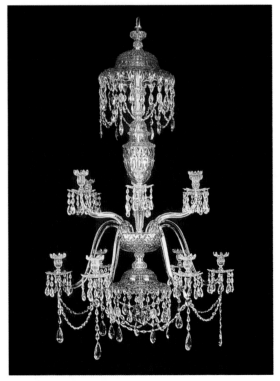

*An Irish George III twelve-light cut-glass chandelier
c.1800; ht 66in (168cm); value code A*

Identification checklist for chandeliers c.1780–1850
1. Do all the elements match?
2. Is there an even number of arms?
3. Are the body and arms correspondingly ornate?
4. Is the plate to which the arms are attached free from holes?
5. Is the chandelier well-balanced?
6. If damaged or reconstructed, are the changes minor?

Chandeliers
Chandeliers have been made for hundreds of years from brass, wood, iron, and more rarely silver, but glass has only been used as a material since the mid-18thC. Not the most efficient form of lighting, because the light is directed upwards, chandeliers

were made as show pieces for public places, churches, large stately homes and palaces. Chandeliers are usually impressive and always expensive: the late 18thC twelve-branch example in the main picture has arms that are arranged to give the effect of a ball of light.

18thC chandeliers

The chandelier in the main picture is typical of those from the late 18thC. On earlier 18thC pieces, the centre column was often made from a series of spheres, and the branches emanated from further down the stem. By the late 18thC the branches were fixed around the middle of the column, usually in two layers. As the branches simply slotted into the central plate, various numbers of lights could be used; the unwanted lights were replaced by arms topped with decorative finials.
* The vase effect in the centre of the column is also typical of late 18thC chandeliers.
* Chandeliers were often damaged, especially while being cleaned, and some degree of replacement is acceptable. Major reconstruction and composite chandeliers should be avoided.

This lantern was designed by Thomas Chippendale c.1760. The flat dish canopy or smoke bell caught the soot created by the light. The dish was necessary because these lights were hung much closer to the ceiling than chandeliers. Smoke bells are still found today especially on oil lights, and are either flat such as the one above, or bell-shaped.
* Many lights have been converted to electricity: a sympathetic conversion can add to value.

This chandelier is late 18thC in style, but also shows Venetian, Bohemian and Irish influences which means it is possibly a composite. The plainness of the drip pans on some of the arms originates from the early 18thC, but the drops and chains are very ornate. The flowers attached to the candlestick arms make cleaning very difficult, and the chandelier is squat in form.

Lamps

Ceiling lights were designed first to hold candles and subsequently oil lights. They were made with narrow frames to create as much light as possible
* The value of hall lanterns lies in the framework. The original glass will add value, but replacement glass will not greatly affect the price.

A huge variety of wall lights were produced, ranging from miniature chandeliers to simple glass and brass cages. This Georgian wall lantern was designed to hold a candlestick, and had a mirror at the back to reflect the light.

145

19THC BRITISH GLASS

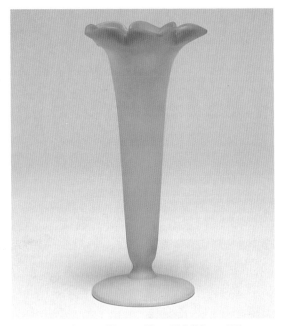

A Queen's Burmese Ware vase, Thomas Webb & Sons , c.1890

The Industrial Revolution had a dramatic effect on the glass-making industry, and a huge variety of glass wares were produced in Britain during the 19thC. The benefit of high quality lead crystal glass, together with a ready supply of low-cost labour, meant that craftsmen were able to experiment with new techniques. British glass received a further boost as glassmakers realized that Continental soda glass was too bright and fragile for industrial production processes.

A relatively affluent middle class grew up in Britain during the Victorian era, and generated a demand for all kinds of decorative arts. Victorian glassware often exhibited a tendency towards over-ornamentation, but many other forms and styles emerged during this period that were admired throughout the world.

Innovation reached its height during the series of international industrial exhibitions in the mid to late 19thC. The Great Exhibition of 1851, held at the Crystal Palace, in London's Hyde Park, set the style for the exhibitions that followed. These events brought together under one roof manufacturers from all over the world.

The exhibitions raised the profile of glassworkers and designers, provided the opportunity for contact between them and a number of potential employers. This created the basis for the integration of glassmaking knowledge, techniques and styles. At the beginning of the century the highest quality glass was made in Britain, many of the most skilled cutters and engravers were Bohemian, and the best gilders and enamellers tended to be French. But by 1900 a pan-European style had developed in addition to national styles, and consequently attribution of work to particular factories is difficult. Marking glass did not become common until the early 20thC; even at the end of the 19thC factory marks were rare, though the artists themselves occasionally signed their work. Many major modern glasshouses were established and thrived during this period, while several older factories and glassmaking centres declined because they failed to innovate, such as the Irish glassmakers.

Many British factories were particularly influential, such as W. H., B. & J. Richardson, Thomas Webb, Stevens & Williams (now Brierley). The scale of these glassworks gave their craftsmen both the opportunity and the resources with which to experiment, and most significant 19thC developments were made in this way.

Developed in the United States in the 1820s, machine-pressed glass was not mass-produced in Britain until the Excise Tax on the weight of glass was repealed in 1845. Many factories started to manufacture pressed glass, and a large number of decorative, functional and inexpensive wares were made, in many colours and styles.

There was a revival in the production of cameo glass in the 19thC. In 1786 the famous Roman artefact the Portland Vase, a white-on-blue cameo, had been brought to England by the Duke of Portland, and inspired by this great piece of craftsmanship Josiah Wedgwood created his Jasper ware. Many glassworkers attempted to copy the vase, and Benjamin Richardson, a Stourbridge manufacturer offered a prize of £1,000 to the first person who could make an exact replia. The process was so complex that a successful copy was not completed until 1876: John Northwood carried out the carving on a blank made by Philip Pargeter, the owner of the Red House Glassworks in Stourbridge, and the whole operation took three years. Other important cameo cutters include Joseph Locke, Alphonse Lecheveral, and most notably George Woodall.

The production of cameo glass in the 19thC was facilitated by the introduction of a technique known as acid-etching. This process used acid (usually hydrofluoric) to eat away at the surface of the glass, and was used to create matte or frosted designs as a form of decoration on its own, but was also used in the preliminary stages of cameo cutting in order to save time.

For the collector there is a huge range of wares available, but as a result condition is all-important. Prices vary to suit every pocket. It is a good idea to visit museums and reputable collectors before buying, to help you choose an area of particular interest. The most valuable items are usually those that have taken the most time to produce, such as some items of cameo glass.

NAILSEA GLASS

A collection of coloured bells
c.1850; ht 10¼–13in (27–33cm); value code (each piece) G

Identification checklist for Nailsea glass bells
1. Does the bell have a coloured, probably decorated body?
2. Does it have a clear handle (coloured ones are more unusual)?
3. Is the handle knopped?
4. Is the bell in two pieces with a plaster of Paris join?
5. Does it have a clapper, or a wire hook for a clapper?
6. Is there any applied decoration?
7. Is the piece made with obvious skill?
8. Does it have purely decorative value?

Nailsea glass
Nailsea glass has become a generic term for a wide range of decorative odds and ends made by glassworkers, for their own profit and sometimes for apprentice tests or guild processions, from the spare glass left in the vat at the end of the day. The Nailsea Glasshouse, near Bristol, established in 1788, made bottle glass and crown window glass; bottles were made in shades of green, and the window glass was clear, pale green. Nailsea items were made in glasshouses in Bristol and the surrounding area, and include bells, such as those in the main picture, flasks, walking sticks, ships, birds of paradise and pipes, and were popular between 1850 and 1900. Nailsea-style decoration describes the looped trails of opaque white or coloured glass found on many of these novelty pieces.

Bells
These are the most frequently-found Nailsea items, usually with clear handles and coloured bodies, although more than half are red. Bells with coloured handles are very rare. The handles and bodies were made as two separate pieces and joined with plaster of Paris. There is often a wire hook embedded in the plaster to take a clapper.
* Bells with clappers do not tend to be more valuable, although they may be more desirable than those without.
* The bells are often decorated: the bodies may feature white filigree rims, ribbing or wrythen moulding, and the handles are sometimes knopped.
* Some copies were made in the 1950s. These tend to be very ornate, and the glass of the body tends to be coarser and thicker than the originals.

Nailsea flasks and pipes usually feature combed, looped or striped decoration, such as this clear flask with white combing. Blue or pink decoration on clear or opaque white bodies is also found. Pipes appear in a variety of shapes and patterns, with elaborate knopped stems.

Colours include dark blue, green and a raspberry-coloured glass known as cranberry. Some witch balls were made with Nailsea-style decoration.

Items resembling witch balls are found in Eastern Europe, but these are used as garden decorations and often have necks.

Other Nailsea glass

* Sailing ships made of filigree glass were made as inexpensive novelties for living rooms. Although these were still called Nailsea glass, they were made in the Midlands, around Birmingham and Stourbridge.

These should only be bought if they have a glass dome, otherwise they get dirty and are extremely difficult to clean. Condition is a very important factor in the value of Nailsea ships.

* Witch balls are large, coloured glass spheres that were often silvered inside giving a metallic effect, and they were hung in windows to repel the evil eye and bring good luck. They have fittings similar to those found on Christmas tree decorations for hanging, and are very fragile.

This clear and opaque white decanter is a good example of the quality of workmanship found in Nailsea pieces. It is delicate and elegantly proportioned, features the characteristic looped decoration, and like most of these items it was intended to be decorative rather than useful.

* A traditional farewell present from a sailor to his sweetheart was a decorative glass rolling pin. Rolling pins were made from the early 18thC onwards, first in crown glass and later coloured; many were made from dark blue Bristol glass. They often featured looped decoration in pink, red or blue, and many were enamelled with flowers and transfer-printed designs.

Walking sticks

Another popular Nailsea product was the walking stick, an item which became surrounded by superstition – they were hung in windows to attract evil spirits and then dusted to remove them from the house.

The example *below* is typical, a standard-size walking stick, made from solid glass with a blue internal twist.

* Glass sticks were also made on the Continent, but were hollow novelties that were designed to be filled with sweets.

CROWN GLASS DUMPS AND OTHER FUNCTIONAL ITEMS

*A Crown glass dump with bubble decoration
c.1850; ht 7in (18cm); value code G*

Identification checklist for Crown glass dumps
1. Does the glass have a pale green tint (dark blue and dark green are unusual)?
2. Does it include bubbles and indentations?
3. Is there any decoration, such as plaster inclusions or a large number of bubbles?
4. Does the dump weigh between 1 and 10lb (0.5–5kg)?
5. Does it have a flat base?
6. Is it in perfect condition?
7. Does the dump look as if it may have come from a mould, such as a sheaf of wheat or a dog shape?

Crown glass
Crown glass was used to make window panes, but as with Nailsea glass (see pp.148–149), workers often used "end of day" glass to make items which they sold privately. Window glass was made by cutting open a bubble of blown glass, attaching it to a rod and spinning it to form a disc which was then cut into small squares. The central square would bear the scar of the rod and was sold off cheaply: these panes are often seen in pub windows.

Dumps
A "dump" is a doorstop, the most frequently-found item made from left-over glass. Dumps, such as the one in the main picture, weigh between 1 and 10lbs (0.5–5kg), and are made from glass that has a green tint; this is the natural colour of the glass which would not be evident in windows because of their relative thinness. They usually feature simple bubble decoration, although some have crude plaster inclusions.

* Due to the nature of their function, dumps in pristine condition are very rare.

Doorstop copies

Some glass factories in the Midlands produced dumps made from the same moulds as cast-iron doorstops. Very occasionally these were made in dark green and dark blue: left-over metal oxides, when available, were thrown into the vat to colour the glass. Moulding was very crude, and bubbles and unintentional indentations are often found.

The most common doorstops are in the shape of sheaves of wheat and dogs, such as this one, which are often found in opposing pairs.
* Damaged pieces should be avoided at all cost.
* A pair of dogs may be worth up to three times as much as a single one.
* Of all Crown glass items, dogs and plain dumps are the most desirable.

Cream pails

The cream pail *below*, was used in a dairy for separating the milk from the cream. Pails are usually large, measuring between 12 and 36in (30.5–91.5cm) in diameter, always have a lip and a folded rim, and are not decorated.
* Large cream pails are rarer and therefore more valuable than more usual-sized examples.

Cloches

Crown glass was also used to make vegetable covers or cloches, that were used in the gardens of country houses.

Cloches also measure between 12 and 36in (30.5–91.5cm) in height – this is a larger example (24in, 60cm), and typically it has a large glass knob on the top.
* Avoid cloches if they are cloudy; this comes from outdoor use and cannot be rectified.
* Other garden accessories made from Crown glass include tubes for growing straight cucumbers, fly and wasp traps, and grape ripeners.

Copies

* Plain dumps and moulded dogs have not been copied. Some coloured doorstops (other than green or blue) exist from the same period, but these cannot correctly be called dumps which are strictly "end of day" items made from left-over glass.
* Modern cloches do exist, but these tend to be made from finer, slightly clearer glass (not the natural green of the originals), and have no imperfections.

JUGS AND EWERS

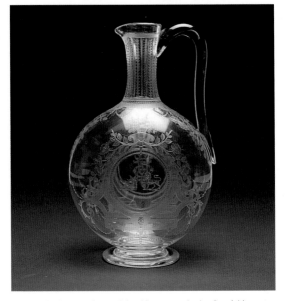

A finely-engraved, armorial wedding presentation jug, Stourbridge c.1860; ht 10¼ in (26cm); value code E.

Identification checklist for late 19thC jugs

1. Has the handle been drawn upwards, with the wider part at the base?
2. Does the jug have a stopper?
3. If there is no stopper, is the inside of the neck smooth?
4. Is the glass free from cloudiness?
5. Does the handle ring?
6. If decorated, is the craftsmanship of good quality?

Jugs

Because of the relative difficulty involved in their production: jug handles were applied hot after the bodies had been finished, producing stresses and weaknesses in the glass. Jugs tend to be rarer than decanters or carafes. Some important mid-19thC jugs were made in a flattened dough-nut shape, such as the one in the main picture. This gave a much greater surface area to decorate, and was ideal for scenes, crests or coats of arms. The date of manufacture of 19thC jugs can be difficult to establish, but many features offer clues.

Dating point

The style of the handle on a Victorian jug can help to give a collector an idea of when a piece was produced. The style of jug handles changed in c.1870: before this time handles were attached at the top and then drawn down. But after 1870 most were made with the handle attached further down the body of the jug and drawn up, and with some modern, handmade exceptions, this still appears to hold true. The reason for this is probably to do with the use of machinery in the manufacturing process.

* While earlier handles may be

seen on jugs produced later than 1870, later handles are never seen on those made before 1870.
* Luxury cut-glass jugs and decanters were made throughout the 19thC, but less expensive wares were not available until after c.1875.

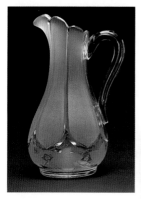

The jug *above* has a typical tall, curved, Victorian form with a high-looped handle that has been drawn down from the top.

On this jug, the lower part of the handle is wider, showing that it has been drawn up from further down the body. This style of handle makes the jug easier to pour.

Stoppers
About 50 per cent of jugs have stoppers which have been "polished in". This means that the neck and the peg of the stopper are bright and not matte in colour like those that have been "ground". Where a jug is found without a stopper it is possible to

feel whether or not it should have one as there will be a slight bump or ledge inside the neck.
* The absence of a stopper where a jug was made to take one will reduce the value of a jug by 25 per cent. However, as jugs were used as serving vessels, stoppers were not often necessary and while the jug narrows at the top fittings are not always felt inside the neck. As a general rule, if the neck is less than a thumb's-width across, the jug should have a stopper.
* Many plain, utilitarian water jugs were made, and were usually straight-sided with a two or three pint capacity. These are quite common and were made at least until the First World War.

Sometimes a jug and a pair of goblets were made to be given as wedding presents, and sold as lemonade or champagne sets – champagne was decanted at this time. The engraved jug and glass *above*, are part of such a set. Complete sets are difficult to find because the jugs were used every day for serving wine and often became worn or damaged, and the glasses were kept for special occasions.

Condition
* Check for damage around the handle joins by tapping the handle: if it does not ring then there is likely to be a crack or a chip.
* The quality of the decoration on a jug is an important determinant of value.
* Avoid jugs with cloudy glass bodies: this is caused by water damage and is difficult to remedy. Ordinary dirt can easily be removed.

MISCELLANEOUS TABLEWARE

Two wine glass coolers
c.1810 and c.1840; ht (both) 4in (10cm); value code H

Identification checklist for early wine glass coolers c.1780–c.1820

1. Is the bowl roughly the same size as a clenched fist (some early, large, glass coolers exist, but these are very rare)?
2. Does the bowl have two lips, on opposite sides of the rim?
3. Is the bowl relatively tall and narrow?
4. Is the piece quite coarse and heavy?
5. Is there wear on the base?
6. Does the bowl feature fairly simple decoration (later pieces are more ornate)?

Wine glass coolers

Wine glass coolers, or rinsers as they are known in the United States, are an unusual item of late 18th and 19thC tableware. They are approximately the same size as a finger bowl with pouring lips on either side of the rim, and they were used to rinse or cool wine glasses between the wines which accompanied each course of a meal. Usually during the 18thC a single glass was used throughout a meal and all those dining rinsed their glasses in a communal silver monteith. From 1780 however, individual wine glass coolers were made; the first examples had a single lip on which to balance the stem of the glass while the bowl was washed. A second lip was then added in

order to make the item symmetrical. In c.1860 Victorian diners began to use a different glass for each wine consumed.

The shape of a wine glass cooler can often be a guide to the date of manufacture:
* the narrow fluting and upright bowl of the cooler in the main picture suggest that it was made

in c.1810, and used to clean the smaller, long-stemmed drinking glasses typical of the time. Older coolers are usually quite coarse and heavy with wear on the base. Early wine coolers were made between c.1780 and c.1820.

* the wider, lower shape of the cooler *below left*, from around 1840, was more appropriate for the larger glasses that were fashionable in the mid-19thC. The decoration on this piece is more elaborate than the other example, which also suggests a later date of manufacture.

Coloured wine glass coolers

Wine glass coolers were also made in coloured glass between 1800 and 1830, in blue, green, amethyst, and more rarely red. Check before buying because copies were made in the 1930s and usually bear a factory mark.

* The price range for wine coolers varies, but all are relatively inexpensive. Sets have no extraordinary value.

Dessert services

Between 1860 and 1890 glass dessert services became popular – previously they had been made from china or porcelain. Often given as gifts, the sets comprised a group of *tazzas* in various sizes, and a set of flat plates.

This *tazza* from c.1860 is a typical high-quality, cut-glass serving dish. It has an ornate foot which was characteristic of expensive Victorian glassware. The surface is 8in (20.3cm) in diameter, and this *tazza* would have been the second largest of the group.

* Be careful not to confuse cut decoration with pressed or moulded *tazzas*, these are more common and less valuable.

* Other *tazzas* were produced during the same period with engraved and gilded decoration.

Pickle jars

Pickle jars first appeared around 1810, and although early examples are rare they had become commonplace by the second half of the century. Although a typical form with a squat body and wide neck, the coloured jar *above*, from around 1870 is rare because most were made from clear glass.

* The quality and price of pickle jars vary enormously – be sure to check the colour and the weight of the metal – but once again all are relatively affordable.

Knife rests

Another unusual piece of glassware, the pair of knife rests *above*, was made by the Belgian company Val St. Lambert in c.1880. Large stands made to support the carving knife and fork are found in Britain in a range of materials. In France and other areas of Europe where the same knife and fork are used throughout the meal, individual rests are used.

* Glass knife rests are inexpensive, were made by most European factories, and are therefore interesting items to collect.

* Collectable rests include those with colour twists (see the top rest *above*), those made by the French manufacturers Baccarat and Lalique, rests with ends carved in the shape of animals and classical figures, and those made from cut glass.

THE GREAT EXHIBITION 1851

*Engraved, red souvenir goblet for the Great Exhibition
c.1851; ht 9in (23cm); value code D*

*** An identification checklist for glassware shown at the
Great Exhibition is inappropriate because of the great
variety of wares displayed.**

The Great Exhibition
"The Great Exhibition of the
Works of Industry of all Nations"
was held in a huge glass and
metal structure designed by
Joseph Paxton, in London's Hyde
Park. The exhibition was opened
by Queen Victoria on 1 May
1851, and over the five months it
was open there were six million
visitors. The commemorative
goblet in the main picture
features an engraving of the
Crystal Palace and the inscription
reads: "Building for the Grand
International Exhibition".

British exhibitors and
techniques
There were 157 exhibitors of
glass from around the world at
this event which marked a water-
shed in glass design. The excise
taxes on the colour and weight of
glass had been abolished in 1845,
and this gave craftsmen more
scope. Most of the items were

documented and can be checked
in contemporary catalogues. The
designs were innovative with few
echoes of past styles. Major
British exhibits included:
* engraved glass by George
Bacchus & Sons, Birmingham
* cut glass of all descriptions,
including furniture, by F. & C.
Osler, Birmingham
* silvered glass by E. Varnish &
Co., London
* engraved, cut and fancy glass by
James Powell & Sons, London
* cut and engraved glass by
Apsley Pellatt & Co., London
* cut, coloured, engraved, and
enamelled opaque glass by
W. H., B. & J. Richardson,
Stourbridge.

F. & C. Osler
As well as their intricate cut glass
furniture and chandeliers (see
p.159), Osler also produced items
with a more "modern", almost
Art Deco style.

The small jug and drinking glass *above*, illustrates the simple form and clean lines that were beginning to be favoured by a number of art critics in Britain at this time, including John Ruskin.

The bulrush engraving in the Neo-Classical style was often used to decorate Osler wares. A number of pieces on display at the Exhibition were purchased by the Parisian museum, the Conservatoire Nationale des Arts et Métiers, as representing the new direction in the production of glassware.

W. H., B. & J. Richardson
Opaque glassware decorated with "Richardson's Vitrified Colours", the firm's patented technique (see pp.158–159), was displayed at the Exhibition, decorated in the Neo-Classical style.

This pair of opaline vases, decorated with brown and black enamels, feature typical Grecian motifs and border designs; they are marked "Richardson's Vitrified", and are further identified by a diamond registration lozenge for 6 July 1847.

The centrepiece of the Great Exhibition was a cut-glass fountain set on a white marble base, also by Osler; the entry in the *Art Journal's* official catalogue reads, "The lightness and beauty as well as the perfect novelty of its design have rendered it the theme of admiration with all visitors". The fountain was 23ft 6in (7.2m) high, and following the Exhibition it was bought by the Maharaja of Puttiala.

Coloured glass
Coloured glass, together with crystal, formed the two main types of glass produced in the 19thC. At the Great Exhibition the British factories showed a spectacular range of colours: Rice Harris of Birmingham, for example, included opal, alabaster, turquoise, amber, canary, topaz, chrysoprase, pink, blue, light and dark ruby, black, brown, green and purple in his display. Flashed, cased and stained glass was also produced by British manufacturers, demonstrating a strong Bohemian influence.

MAJOR VICTORIAN MANUFACTURERS

Gilt and silvered vase attributed to Jules Barbe, possibly Thomas Webb Stourbridge, c.1890; ht 9¾ in (25cm); value code D

* An identification checklist for Victorian glassware is inappropriate because of the variety of different designs available.

Victorian Manufacturers

The Victorian period was probably one of the most inventive for techniques and styles of glass manufacture, and most of them have survived (sometimes in a modified form) up to the present day. Some skills, however, have been lost due to their unsuitability for mass production, high cost or the introduction of new methods. Many of the major manufacturers introduced complex, patented techniques during this period.

Thomas Webb & Sons (1856–present)

Founded in Stourbridge, Thomas Webb & Sons began to produce high-quality glassware in 1856, and are best-known for cameo, Burmese ware and rock crystal-style glass. As well as having their own specialist craftsmen, Webb also employed freelance glass decorators, such as the Frenchman Jules Barbe, who is thought to have designed the vase in the main picture. Barbe worked mainly on glass and china, often in an Oriental style with paste goldwork.

The gilded and silvered decoration on this piece is highly elaborate, as each process would have to be carried out separately, and would have taken around two to three weeks to complete.
* Other than cameo glass, pieces by Webb are only occasionally marked.

W.H., B. & J. Richardson

W.H., B. & J. Richardson was established in 1829 by William Haden Richardson, and his two brothers, Benjamin and Johnathan, at a glassworks in Wordsley, near Stourbridge. The firm is famous for its patented designs and high-quality wares.

The firm produced glass using many patented techniques, including Bohemian-style glass with panels that were alternately colour-flashed and clear, and then engraved. This amber vase engraved with a floral design is a typical example. All the items in this style were serving pieces, such as vases, decanters and claret jugs. While amber is the most usual colour, red, green and purple are also found.

Vitrified Colours
Another famous Richardson patent was known as "Vitrified Colours". Items made using this technique were displayed at the Great Exhibition. The process involved transfer printing and firing a black or coloured pattern onto the glass body (usually opaque). Sometimes the enamels were hand-painted onto the body although this is less common.

Richardson pieces are often marked; the full mark that is found on the base of an item is shown here, but many are marked just "Richardson". Sometimes a diamond registration mark, known as a lozenge, may also be included.

E. Varnish & Co.
Silvered glass was patented by Edward Varnish and Frederick Hale Thompson in 1849. The interior of this double-walled glassware was lined with silver creating a mirrored effect, and the gap in the base was then sealed with a disc showing their trade mark.

Silvered glassware such as this cup was produced for only a short period, at the time of the international exhibitions.

* Varnish wares are usually sealed and marked; do not buy a piece if the seal has been lost, as the silvered surface will deteriorate if it is not airtight.

F. & C. Osler (1807–1922)
This Birmingham-based manufacturer, which also had showrooms in London and Calcutta, produced glass of exceptional quality which was usually very heavily cut.

Osler also made speciality glass furniture which was especially popular in the Far East, such as this cut-glass occasional table c.1875. The style follows the Victorian furniture of the period made from other media, such as wood and papier mâché.

BRISTOL GLASS

A pair of gilded, pint-size Bristol spirit bottles
c.1800; 8in (20cm); value code D

Identification checklist for Bristol spirit bottles
1. Is the glass blue or green (other colours are less common)?
2. Does the bottle have a capacity of one imperial pint?
3. Is the body free from cut decoration?
4. Is there gilded decoration on the stopper and body of the decanter?
5. Does the body have a gilded label identifying the contents, and the stopper the first initial?
6. Does the gilding have a smooth, "old" gold matte finish?

Bristol glass
The term "Bristol" when applied to glass has come to encompass all blue, green and amethyst glass made in Britain from the end of the 18th until the middle of the 19thC. In fact, only a small group of gilded blue items are known to have been made in Bristol. These pieces include decanters, finger bowls, wine glass coolers, and toilet or perfume bottles that are signed *I. Jacobs, Bristol*. Isaac

Jacobs is known to have worked as a gilder in Bristol in the late 18th and early 19thC. Although signed items are rare, their shapes and styles can help to identify the origin of unsigned pieces.

Spirit bottles and decanters
Coloured glass of this type does display certain characteristics. Decanters or spirit bottles, such the ones in the main picture, most commonly made in blue,

were often gilded with a label identifying the contents: usually rum, brandy or Hollands (gin). Stoppers are frequently gilded with the first letter, "R", "B" or "H". Bristol decanters are generally pint sized; larger ones are rare (if gilded they were made to hold wine). 80 per cent of decanters are blue and green, while amethyst is less common.
* Ungilded pint-sized decanters are uncommon. They should be examined against a strong light to check for shadows left from rubbed or faded gilding.
* Gilding has a smooth "old" gold matte finish; regilding will appear too bright and slightly grainy and will dramatically affect the value.
* Gilding is common on serving pieces such as decanters, but not on drinking glasses.

Many Bristol cruet bottles were made in decanter form and were decorated in a similar way. They were often made in sets, and presented in plated holders. This small cruet bottle exhibits all the features mentioned above. Used to hold "kayan" or cayenne pepper, the gilding on the stopper, lip and body of this cruet bottle are all in good condition.

Drinking glasses
The most common colour for Bristol drinking glasses is green, and they were meant to hold port rather than wine. They were made in a huge variety of shades, ranging from grass green to turquoise. It is almost impossible to match the colours of Bristol glasses unless they were made as part of a set.

Bristol drinking glasses are always about 4in (10cm) high and all sections are made in one single colour. Common bowl shapes are the drawn trumpet featured, drawn funnel and tulip. The stem of this glass is knopped, but stems are more commonly plain.
* Amethyst drinking glasses are rare, but when found usually have drawn trumpet bowls. The colours are delicate and show no trace of red when held up to the light: Victorian copies have a plum colour when tested in this way.
* Blue drinking glasses should be treated with caution as a large number of these were made during the first half of the 20thC. Generally these glasses are larger than the older ones, have unusual shapes, and a very thin metal (glass body). They do, however, have snapped-off pontils which can be confusing.

A less common colour than blue or green, this amethyst finger bowl is a good example of the rich shades found in Bristol glass.
* The characteristic, dark blue Bristol glass was made using cobalt oxide from Cornwall.
* Green Bristol glass became unfashionable and disappeared after c.1850.

Value
* Late 18thC Bristol glass is rare and expensive, but later pieces are affordable.

COLOURED GLASS

Victorian coloured drinking glass
c.1850; ht 4½in (11.5cm); value code H

Identification checklist for coloured Victorian drinking glasses, c.1860–1880

1. Does the glass measure up to 4½in (11.5in) high?
2. Does the glass have a coloured bowl and a clear stem?
3. Is the bowl red, green, or shades of blue, amber or amethyst?
4. Does the bowl have a rounded base?
5. Is the bowl taller than it is wide?
6. Is there a collar under the bowl?
7. Is there a ground-out pontil mark or tool mark on the base?
8. Is the glass sturdy with a relatively thick body (later versions have thinner bodies)?

Coloured glass
Coloured glass is usually created by the addition of a metallic oxide to the glass mix. Many colours created in the 19thC were made using metals that are now known to be extremely dangerous, such as uranium and arsenic, and are therefore never made today. Colours found during the 19thC include green and red which were relatively common, while amethyst and blue (in various shades) were quite rare.

Late Victorian drinking glasses
The shape of the glass in the main picture is typical of drinking glasses from the second half of 19thC, used for white wine or pale sherry. Made in glasshouses in London and the Midlands, they are different from "Bristol" wares made at the beginning of the 19thC (see pp.160–161). Glasses such as this one are average quality; higher quality pieces usually feature cut or engraved decoration.

* Glasses made c.1860–1880 are characterized by a collar under the bowl, as seen on the green glass in the main picture and the red glass *below right*. The blue glass, *below left*, with no collar, was probably made later
* The combination of clear and coloured glass is typical of late Victorian glasses.

* Copies of coloured glasses exist, especially red, but have much thinner bodies than the originals.

Colouring agents

The most common metals used to produce particular colours were as follows:
* red: gold, copper, selenium
* orange: carbon, sulphur
* yellow: iron, cerium, uranium, silver
* green: iron, cobalt, chromium
* blue: cobalt, copper
* violet: manganese, nickel
* white/opaline: arsenic, tin, flourspar, calcium, phosphate.

* The resulting colour was still liable to vary, however, depending on factors including the other constituents of the glass, the temperature of the furnace, and the general nature of the chemical used to colour the glass.

Uranium glass

Glass made with uranium which produced a bright, acid yellow, was produced in Bohemia from c.1830, where an opaque apple-green glass, known as chrysoprase was also produced (see pp.46–47). Chrysoprase was the name used by Stevens & Williams to describe a pale yellow glass with an amber tint, such as the faceted drinking glass from around 1880 shown *below*.

* Early Bohemian pieces are usually larger and heavier, and are more desirable than later British-made uranium wares.

Burmese glassware

Burmese glass, characterized by a body colour which graduates from yellow to pale pink, was originally produced in the United States in 1886 by the Mount Washington Glass Company. In Britain in the same year this style of glass was patented by Thomas Webb & Sons under the name "Queen's

Burmese", so-called because it was favoured by Queen Victoria.
* Some pieces were made with gilded and enamelled decoration (see *below*), and the best pieces have acid-stamped factory marks. Pieces by Webb are most collectable of this type of glass but similar wares were made by other factories.

This distinctive colour was created using a combination of gold and uranium oxides, together with sodium nitrate: the glass changed colour when reheated quickly, as seen on the fringe of the bowl *left*. Burmese wares were mainly ornamental pieces such as vases.

19THC ENGRAVED GLASS

*Small claret jug engraved with roses, probably by W. J. Muckley
c.1860; ht 10in (25cm); value code F.*

Identification checklist for 19thC engraved glass
1. Is the glass body high quality?
2. Is the decoration well drawn and detailed?
3. Is the engraved subject desirable (such as an animal, a building, armorial, commemorative or floral)?
4. Is the design engraved *into* the glass and not etched *onto* the surface?
5. If signed, is there an engraved signature and not a acid-stamped mark?
6. Is the piece in good condition?
7. Is the pontil ground out?

Wheel engraving
Wheel cutting and engraving on glass are carried out using the same machinery, but while cutting the piece is held under the wheel so that the weight is pressing downwards, and for engraving it is held above the wheel. Almost all 19thC engraving was produced by copper wheels (varying between ½in (1cm) and 4in (10cm) in diameter), together with a fine abrasive paste (usually a mixture of oil and emery). The fashion in the 19thC for engraving began around 1830, but was given a boost by the Great Exhibition of 1851 (see pp.156–157). Meanwhile the popularity of cut glass declined.

Subjects
Typical motifs included fruiting vines, but some pieces were engraved with political and commemorative subjects.

The Caroline Forever rummer *below* from c.1820, was engraved in support of Caroline of Brunswick, the estranged wife of George IV (formerly the Prince Regent). Following his accession, Caroline returned from a tour of Europe to claim her place as Queen, but on the King's instruction was tried by the House of Lords for conduct of a "most licentious character", in order to obtain a divorce.

mentioned above will be extremely valuable, especially if signed. But some engraved pieces of a lower quality were also produced, such as this bar jug decorated with ferns. These are worth considerably less.
* Value depends on the subject and the quality of the engraving.
* Condition is very important: cracks can reduce the value of a piece by 95 per cent.

The best engraving usually features figures of animals; other desirable subjects include flowers, buildings, historical commemorative designs, and important coats of arms.
* The most common subjects are poorly drawn ferns and stars.
* Some plant subjects can help to date the pieces on which they appear: ivy and convulvulus are early Victorian, c.1850; classic floral motifs, c.1860; ferns and grasses, c.1870.

Craftsmen

Some of the most important engravers of the period were W. J. Muckley who engraved the jug in the main picture, the Northwood family, Fritsche, Palme and Woodhall.
* Many artists signed their work, sometimes on the base, but more commonly within the decoration itself. Treat signatures with caution: if genuine they will greatly increase the value of a piece, but dubious signatures do exist.
* A genuine signature will be engraved into the glass; an acid-stamped mark does not constitute a signature on an engraved piece.

Quality

The quality of engraved pieces varies enormously. Items engraved by the artists

Diamond-point engraving

There is a group of average quality, diamond-point engraved items, including tavern rummers and tumblers. This technique involves scratching a design onto

the surface of the glass with a diamond-tipped stylus. This 19thC rummer has been diamond-point engraved with a ship, and the motto "He who fights and runs away, lives to fight another day", and was probably engraved to order at a port for a sailor embarking on a voyage. These personalized items can be an interesting area in which to collect.

ACID-ETCHED GLASS

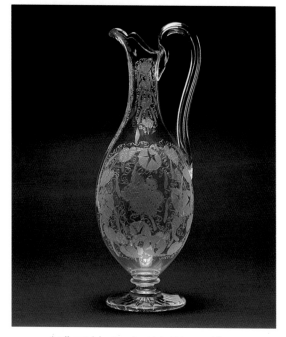

A tall, crystal champagne jug etched with leaves and flowers c.1870; ht 13in (33cm); value code F

Identification checklist for 19thC acid-etched glass
1. Does the decoration appear on the surface, and not scratched into the glass?
2. Does the surface have a matte or frosted finish?
3. Is the decoration high quality and innovative, with great attention to detail?
4. Is the decoration a desirable subject (such as Neo-Classical or floral)?
5. If there is any additional engraved decoration, does it feature details of a place, a crest or a coat of arms?
6. Is the body of the glass of high quality?
7. Is there a ground-out pontil mark?

Acid etching
Acid etching was invented around 1830, and for some years was regarded as a novelty. Expensive acid-etched presentation items were made, often with a little cut or hand-made embellishment. The champagne jug in the main picture features engraved stems as well as acid-etched leaves and flowers. Many of these pieces were displayed at the major international exhibitions held between 1850 and 1880.

Technique
If a glass surface is exposed to acid, usually hydrofluoric, it gives a satin matte or frosted finish.

Early acid-etched glass was made by creating a pattern in outline using acid, and then "obscuring" or shading the solid parts of the design by hand using engraving tools. The glass in the main picture is a high quality example. Items made in this way are usually highly detailed and better quality than those made later using the entirely acid-based technique.

Later acid etching involved coating a glass surface with an acid-resistant substance (usually wax or later, gutta-percha), cutting or engraving a pattern through the coating, and then dipping the glass into hydrofluoric acid which eats into the exposed surface giving the design a matte finish. Pieces such as the jug *above*, tend to be less desirable: patterns often lack imagination, there is a lack of attention to detail and less depth to the finished work.
* This type of decoration is even and effective, but is less sought-after because it is mass-produced.

Subjects
* The most desirable acid-etched wares are large pieces such as jugs, decanters and goblets, decorated with classical scenes: John Northwood, for example, drew scenes from the *Iliad*. Another classical subject is *anthenium* (a honeysuckle pattern that appeared around Greek cornices).
* Less desirable decoration includes simple geometric designs, badly-drawn flowers and ferns, and incomplete patterns.
* Sometimes etched items feature engraved names, dates and crests: details of places, crests and coats of arms enhance the value of a piece; names, initials and monograms will reduce the value.

Acid-cut cameo glass
Acid etching or cutting was used as a first stage in the production of commercial cameo glass (see pp.168–169) and in some cases was used to cut cameo patterns, the vase *above* is a good example of acid-cut faux cameo.

In 1857 Benjamin Richardson took out a patent on a mixture of sulphuric and hydrofluoric acid, which gave a brighter, etched finish. In c.1867 John Northwood developed a formula that diluted hydrofluoric acid with potassium or sodium carbonate, producing a substance he called "white acid". This created a matte finish, and meant that shading no longer had to be carried out by hand.
* Pieces made using this technique can be distinguished from hand-cut cameos by the softer lines and poor background finish left by the acid.

Etching is sometimes found on coloured glass, such as this vase. This is unusual, but is not necessarily more desirable because the designs are less distinct.

CAMEO GLASS

A George Woodall cameo vase showing the goddess Diana c.1880; ht 7½ in (19.5cm); value code B

Identification checklist for 19thC cameo glass
1. Does the design stand out in relief from the body of the piece?
2. Are there two or more layers of glass visible in the decoration?
3. Are the edges of the design sharp and clean?
4. Has the piece been hand cut?
5. Is the background smooth?
6. Is the design itself intricate and detailed?
7. If signed, does the signature appear on the base or within the decoration itself?
8. If there is an important mark, is the piece of commensurate quality?
9. If there is a geometric border at the top or the base, is the pattern complete?

Cameo glass
Cameo glass was first produced in Roman times, but the technique fell into disuse until the beginning of the 19thC when some very important pieces were made. The most valuable pieces are signed, and figural subjects, such as on the vase in the main picture by George Woodall, are most desirable. Signatures are found on the base, or within the design itself, as here where it appears in the bottom corner.

British cameos
The major British manufacturers of cameo in the 19thC were Thomas Webb, W.H., B. & J. Richardson, and Stevens & Williams, and were all based in the Midlands. Glass bodies

known as "blanks" were made by local glassworks, and carved by the companies' skilled craftsmen.

Faux cameo

Cameo glass made in the 20thC is generally acid cut using hydrochloric acid, and is known as "faux cameo". Some acid cutting was used in the 19thC to produce commercial items, but does not usually affect the overall value as the detailed work was still done by hand.

Faux cameo made using the acid technique are easy to identify because the edges of the design are soft, and the background is "roughed" or heavily textured, and not smooth as on 19thC originals.

George Woodall is the most renowned 19thC cameo engraver, and produced most of his work for Thomas Webb & Sons. This cameo plaque is attributed to him although, unlike the vase in the main picture, it is not signed.
* A signature can enhance the value of a piece by 25 per cent.

The small vase by Richardson's, *below left*, engraved with a floral design, is typical of the sort of item made in 19thC cameo glass. Scent bottles were also popular, and often appear with a butterfly or small bird on the reverse.

Technique

* Cameo is produced from two or more layers of different-coloured glass which are cut away from the base vessel leaving the subject standing out in relief. Most cameo glass comprises a coloured body with a white overlay, although up to four layers of different colours may occur.

* Different-coloured glass cools at different rates and this can cause cracking, hence, unfinished pieces are not uncommon.
* The unfinished cameo vase *above*, is typical with blurred edges on the design. Whilst collectable, pieces such as this are considerably less valuable.

Beware

* In recent years pieces have appeared with fake marks: experience will tell if the quality of the cameo is commensurate with the level of craftsmanship suggested by the mark. Seek advice if there is any doubt.
* It is possible to check for any damage such as internal cracks, which will dramatically affect value, by holding the piece up to a strong light.
* Check that an item has not been reduced at the top or the base in order to disguise chips or other damage: geometric borders often appear on cameo pieces, and patterns will be incomplete if any restoration has been attempted.

BRITISH PRESSED GLASS

*A Sowerby spill vase in yellow vitro-porcelain glass
c.1879; ht 4¼ in (10cm); value code H*

Identification checklist for Sowerby's vitro-porcelain glass
1. Does the piece have a glossy, opaque surface?
2. Are mould lines visible?
3. Do the pressed patterns show up clearly in relief?
4. Is there a trade mark?
5. Is there a patent registration mark?

British pressed glass
In Britain it was not until the
1830s that the first glass made
purely by pressing, rather than a
combination of blowing and
pressing, appeared and was produced on a commercial scale.
The development of the
technique was delayed by the
excise tax, which taxed glass on
the weight of the raw materials.
In spite of the potential savings
offered by the mass production of
press-moulded glass, the weight
of the product, when compared
with blown glass, made it
relatively expensive to produce.
The tax was repealed in 1845,
and wide-scale production began
shortly afterwards.

Technique
Pressing glass was, in essence, a
simple process: instead of being
blown by hand, and shaped either
freely or in a wooden mould, the
glass was shaped with a press and
iron moulds. First the glass was
gathered from the crucible using
a blowing iron and dropped into

the mould (a sufficient quantity
was cut from the rod with shears).
Next a plunger was used to press
the plastic mass, so that after
cooling slightly the object
retained the shape of the mould
on one surface, and the plunger
on the other. The item was
removed from the mould and
placed back in a part of the furnace known as the glory hole, and
this process, called fire polishing,
melted away any imperfections
left by the mould, leaving a
bright surface.

Manufacturers
Press moulding on a commercial
scale began in the Midlands and
was adopted by many factories in
the north of England. Few
London-based firms adopted the
technique.
* The three most famous
manufacturers of pressed glass in
Britain were John Sowerby's
Ellison Glassworks, George
Davidson & Co. of Gateshead-
on-Tyne, and Henry Greener &
Co. of Sunderland.

Sowerby (1847–1972)

Established in the early 1800s, Sowerby began producing pressed glass in 1847. Products were patented from 1872 and the trade mark was introduced in 1876. One of their most famous patented wares was vitro-porcelain, made from 1877, which resembled china: a yellow vitro-porcelain vase is shown in the main picture. Other colours included cream (known as "Patent Queen's Ivory Ware"), white (called "Opal"), turquoise and Aesthetic Green. Marbled colours (known as "Malachite") were also produced.

Commemorative pieces such as this amber plate celebrating Queen Victoria's Golden Jubilee in 1887 were made by many factories specializing in the production of pressed glass.

George Davidson & Co. (established 1867)

George Davidson at the Teams Glass Works in Gateshead produced many patented designs, including blue and yellow (known as "Primrose") "Pearline" glass that was introduced in 1889. They also manufactured a full range of functional, clear and coloured glassware, including dishes, egg-cups, jars, ash-trays, jugs and flower pots.

Henry Greener & Co. (established 1858)

After learning his trade in Gateshead, Henry Greener returned to his native Sunderland and went into partnership with the owner of the Wear Flint Glassworks. Greener produced good-quality clear and coloured glass and many commemoratives.
* His characteristic beaded lettering was copied on the Continent, but these pieces are unmarked and of inferior quality.

Collecting

When beginning a collection it is important to remember the following:
* Only buy marked pieces as this will identify the manufacturer and the date of a piece.
* Avoid damaged wares.
* Ornate pieces are more collectable than plain ones.
* Coloured pieces are desirable, especially colours that were unpopular in the 19thC, and therefore not widely produced.
* Commemorative pieces are collectable, particularly those celebrating less well-known events.
* Early items of pressed glass, although interesting in terms of the development of press moulding in Britain, are not as collectable as later, more sophisticated wares.

John Derbyshire & Co. (1873–1876)

Established at Salford in Manchester, John Derbyshire's glassworks specialized in decorative, press-moulded wares. He produced a wide variety of registered and marked designs that are easily identifiable and widely collected.

Derbyshire also produced pressed glass models such as this opaque, black Sphinx, *left*, that is marked 9 March 1876. Other figures include a lion based on Sir Edwin Landseer's statues in Trafalgar Square, Punch and Judy, and Britannia.

VICTORIAN FANCY GLASS

*A four-trumpet épergne with a mirror base and trailed, thread decoration
c.1875; ht 12in (30cm); value code E.*

Identification checklist for Victorian épergnes
1. Do all the sections fit together securely?
2. Is each section free from damage?
3. Are there no spare holes in the frame or base?
4. If the épergne has a mirror base, is it in good
condition?
5. If the glass is coloured, are all the sections the same
shade?
6. If there is any trailed decoration, is it complete?
7. If the épergne has a metal collar, is it free from
damage?

Epergnes
An épergne was originally a centrepiece with several sections,
used to hold desserts and fruit.
By the Victorian period, however,
it had become a table centrepiece
for flowers. The example in the
main picture appeared in Silbert
& Flemming's household goods
catalogue in the mid-1870s.
Silbert & Flemming were important late 19thC retailers who specialized in mail order.

It is usually possible to dismantle épergnes: the central vase of
this épergne unscrews and then
the other sections can be lifted
out. While this made cleaning
easier, it also meant that pieces
were often lost. Also made in
coloured glass, some épergnes
comprised a metal frame into
which the sections were slotted.
Some ornate Victorian épergnes
make impressive centrepieces,
even without flowers.

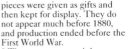

* It is important that every element of an épergne is in good condition, and before buying it is wise to take the épergne apart to check both quality and completeness.
* When coloured (red is the most usual), check that all the sections match: later additions will be a different shade.
* There should be no spare holes for arms and vases in the base plate, this would indicate a missing part.
* Some épergnes have mirror bases, such as the one in the main picture, and these should be in good condition for the épergne to be valuable.

pieces were given as gifts and then kept for display. They do not appear much before 1880, and production ended before the First World War.
* These wares are mainly associated with glasshouses in the Midlands and the north of England, but it is possible that some were imported from Bohemia.
* Jam and sugar bowls are relatively inexpensive to collect, and groups of items can make an effective display.

Fancy jam and sugar bowls such as this one were very popular in the 19thC, and were produced in many different colours, forms and sizes. This typical example, made from orange, heat-sensitive glass cased in clear glass, has an applied fancy border and ornate handle. It is likely that these

This jug gives a good idea of the Victorian taste for ornate decoration, with a trailed thread body, engraved with flowers that have been filled in with gilt and then fired. More usually produced in France, this piece is unusual because it was made in London, c.1890.
* Before buying check that the gilding is in good condition.
* It is important not to wash gilded wares in detergent as this can damage the decoration.

Samples
Another interesting and fairly inexpensive area in which to collect is travellers' sample wares. These were made by manufacturers in many glassmaking centres, not just those in Britain, as high

quality miniatures for salesmen to show to prospective buyers.
* Items are not usually more than 3in (7.6cm) high but often feature elaborate cutting or engraving.
* Manufacturing marks rarely appear.

These three items, the tallest of which measures 2.5in (6.3cm), demonstrate the range of forms available. The water jug *left*, was made either in Stourbridge or London, and the cut, uranium-glass goblet and decanter, were probably made in Bohemia.

SCENT BOTTLES

A pair of green-tinted scent bottles
c.1765; ht 1½ in (3.7cm); value code C

Identification checklist for 18thC scent bottles
1. Is the bottle well-made and carefully finished?
2. Does the glass body feature cut or gilded decoration?
3. If coloured, is the body blue, green, opaque white or (occasionally) amethyst?
4. Does the scent bottle have a metal cap made from silver or silver gilt, that fits over a glass stopper?
5. If there is a metal cap, does it screw on to the bottle?
6. Is the glass stopper air-tight?
7. If the stopper is not metal-topped, is the top the same colour as the body of the scent bottle?
8. Is the bottle in good condition?

18thC scent bottles
The first British-made scent bottles appeared at the beginning of the 18thC. Early examples followed European designs and were flat in shape, but had characteristic British features such as heavy, lead crystal bodies with cut decoration. Some were engraved with English inscriptions. British-style scent bottles began to be made in the mid-18thC in a variety of colours other than clear glass, including blue, white, pale green and occasionally amethyst. Bottles were often made in pairs to go

inside a travelling case: one for perfume and one to hold smelling salts. Smelling salts (a mixture of ammonia, menthol, eucalyptol and lavender), were used to revive people when feeling faint. The case belonging to the bottles in the main picture is made of shagreen (shark skin leather).
* Pairs of scent bottles are valuable, and those with cases are worth even more.

James Giles (1718–1780)
Scent bottles were expensive items, and were often decorated by leading craftsmen, such as the

London-based decorator James Giles, who also worked on porcelain. The bottles were usually made in the Bristol and Staffordshire glassmaking areas, and brought to London to be decorated. James Giles, who decorated the bottles in the main picture, had a workshop in Berwick Street, in London's Soho, and produced high-quality gilding and enamelling. Gilding often appeared over cut decoration in many styles; the most desirable subjects include exotic birds and Chinoiserie subjects.
* Condition is a very important determinant of value.

19thC scent bottles

Towards the end of the Georgian period a large number of scent and smelling salt bottles were made for use at home rather than when travelling, such as the Regency example *below*. These have a unique style, and do not resemble any contemporary shape.

period (with the exception of inkwells, but these always have plain tops unlike scent bottles).
* Scent and smelling salt bottles are almost impossible to tell apart, but in terms of value this is not important.

This unusual amethyst scent bottle features typically Irish cutting; Anglo-Irish cut styles are also common (see pp.134–135). The combination of the squat shape and heavy cutting is found only on scent bottles from this

Many Victorian scent bottles copied the gothic shapes that were popular during that period such as the one *above*. Once again the quality is very high and the decoration is opulent. Many 19thC scent bottles were coloured, later ones were often made with silver mounts. More flamboyantly decorated bottles were imported from France or Bohemia, and mounts added by retailers in this country.
* Late 19thC scent bottles often have hinged lids; earlier examples tend to have screw-on caps.
* Double-ended scent bottles can be found, with one section for perfume and another for smelling salts, with a different patented fastening device for each end.

Cameo scent bottles

The revival in the production of cameo glass (see pp.168–169) in Britain at the end of the 19thC

stimulated the manufacture of a number of elaborate scent bottles by the firms of Thomas Webb and Stevens & Williams.

Webb employed many highly skilled cameo cutters, including George and Thomas Woodall. This scent bottle, with realistic flower decoration, illustrates the quality of workmanship found on the firm's cameo pieces.

GLOSSARY

Acid etching Technique involving treatment of glass with acid, giving a matte or frosted finish.

Annealing Slow cooling of hot glass which reduces internal stresses that may cause cracking once glass is cold.

Baluster 18thC drinking glass with a stem based on the baluster, a form derived from Renaissance architecture.

Balustroid A taller, lighter form of baluster.

Biedermeier A bourgeois style that influenced all the decorative arts in Germany c.1825–1840; *Biedermeier* glass was characterized by the quality and range of its colours.

Blowing A technique of producing glass vessels by blowing a molten mass of glass, or gather, through a blowpipe, either freehand or into a mould.

Cameo glass Decorative carved, cased or flashed glass with two or more different-coloured layers, so that the carved design stands out in relief.

Core-forming Technique of producing a glass vessel by shaping trails of molten glass over a core usually made from mud or clay, and fusing them together in a furnace; the core is scraped out when cool.

Cristallo Type of soda glass developed in 15thC Venice, made with soda derived from the ashes of the barilla plant.

Crizzling Where an imbalance in the glass batch has caused the surface of the glass to become fogged by a network of tiny cracks.

Crown glass Sheet glass primarily used for window panes, produced by cutting open a bubble of blown glass, attaching it to a rod and spinning to form a flat disc which was then cut into squares.

Cullet Pieces of glass added to the glass batch to act as a flux.

Daumenglas A traditional German cylindrical or barrel-shaped beaker.

Diamond-point engraving Line drawing on a glass surface using a diamond or metal point; designs comprising a series of dots rather than lines using this type of tool are called stipple engraving.

Eiserot See *Schwarzlot*.

Enamelling Decorative technique using coloured powdered glass mixed with an oily substance, that is painted onto the glass and reheated to fuse the design to the surface.

Faceting Technique used to decorate curved glass surfaces by grinding to create flat, geometric sections.

Façon de Venise French, meaning "in the Venetian style", used to describe high quality, Venetian-influenced glassware made in Europe during the 16th–17thC.

Faïence Substance made from finely-ground quartz (a form of silica) covered with a glass-like, vitreous glaze.

Filigrana Italian, meaning "thread-grained"(called filigree in English), used to describe many variations of a decorative style which incorporates threads of (usually opaque white) glass inside a clear glass body in a variety of lattice patterns.

Flashed A method of colouring glass which involves applying a thin layer of coloured glass to a vessel, either by painting or dipping it into a pot of colourant; flashed glass can be carved to produce a less expensive version of overlay glass.

Flux An alkaline substance added to the glass batch to aid the fusion of the ingredients.

Gather The mass of molten glass that is attached to the end of a blowpipe or pontil rod before a vessel is formed.

Gilding A technique of glass decoration that involves painting the glass surface with gold leaf, gold dust or gold paint and then firing to fix the design.

Historismus European revival, c.1870, of the production of old Venetian and traditional German glass forms from the 15th and 16thC.

Humpen Tall, cylindrical German beer glass made from the mid-16thC to the 18thC.

Hyalith Opaque black glass, resembling basalt, invented by Count von Buquoy in 1817.

"In front of the kiln" Phrase used to describe applied decoration added by hand to a glass object while it is still hot.

Jacobite glasses 18thC glassware engraved in support of the Jacobite pretenders to the English throne.

Kick Indentation in the base of a glass vessel where the pontil rod is attached.

Knops Swellings, which can be solid or hollow, that occur in a variety of forms on glass stems.

Kuttrolf Antique German bottle for spirits such as schnapps, with a large surface area for cooling.

Lacy glass Type of American pressed glass with a stipple-engraved background that gives a lacy effect.

Lampwork Glass that is blown or manipulated from clear or coloured glass rods over a blow lamp or torch.

Lattimo From the Italian *latte* meaning "milk"; an opaque white glass made by adding bone ash or tin oxide to the glass batch.

Latticino Or *latticinio*, Italian; other terms used to describe *filigrana*.

Lead crystal Glass made using a large proportion of lead oxide that was not vulnerable to crizzling, first made by George Ravenscroft in the late 17thC.

Lithyalin Marbled, opaque, usually red, glass created by Friedrich Egermann to resemble semi-precious stones.

Marvering An ancient technique where hot threads of softened glass are rolled over a flat surface to smooth and fuse the glass, and to fix trailed decoration.

Metal Term used to describe hot or cold glass.

Millefiori Italian, meaning "a thousand flowers"; used to describe mosaic patterns created by horizontal sections of rods of coloured glass often found in paperweights.

Mould blowing See *blowing*.

Nailsea glass Items of novelty glass, such as walking sticks, flasks and bells, made near Bristol in the 18th and 19thC.

Ormolu Gilded bronze decoration.

Overlay glass Also known as cased glass; a technique in which a glass body is covered by one or more different-coloured outer layers that may be carved to produce a design in relief.

Paraison Bubble of molten glass on the end of a pontil rod or blowpipe that has been partially inflated.

Pontil rod Rod that is attached to the base of a vessel to hold it steady while it is finished, after it has been blown.

Press-moulded glass Technique that involves pouring molten glass into a metal mould and pressing it to the sides using a metal plunger; a mechanized version of this process was first developed in the United States in c.1820.

Prunts Decorative technique comprising blobs of glass applied to a glass surface.

Rock crystal engraving Form of engraving where a clear glass surface is highly polished to imitate the mineral rock crystal.

Roemer Traditional German drinking vessel with an ovoid bowl and a cylindrical stem with applied prunts and a spreading foot.

Rubinglas German, "ruby glass"; richly-coloured red glass created by adding copper or gold oxide to the glass mix.

Rummer 19thC English low drinking goblet, traditionally used for drinking rum and water.

Schwarzlot 17thC German technique of freehand painting on glass using translucent black enamel; an iron-red enamel called *eiserot* was also used.

Soda glass Glass made using sodium carbonate as a flux; sodium carbonate can be derived from various sources, see *cristallo*.

Staining A method of colouring glass by painting the surface with metal oxide, and reheating to fix the colour.

Stipple engraving see *diamond-point engraving*.

Tazza Italian "cup"; an ornamental cup or dish with a foot used to serve food, but also for decoration.

Tear Drop-shaped air bubble enclosed in a glass, usually the stem.

Trailing Decorative technique where strands of glass are drawn out from a gather and trailed over a glass surface.

Uranium glass Glass coloured with uranium, first developed in Germany where *Annagelb* (yellow-green) and *Annagrün* (green) were produced. Another type of uranium glass produced in Germany was an opaque, apple-green glass called chrysoprase.

Vetro a fili Italian "thread glass"; a type of *filigrana*. Other types include *vetro a reticello* (glass with a small network); *vetro a retortoli* (glass with a twist); *vetro di trino* (lace glass).

Waldglas German "forest glass"; green-coloured glass made with a potash (potassium carbonate) flux that is derived from the ashes of burned wood or ferns. In France this type of glass is known as *verre de fougère*.

SELECTED DESIGNERS AND MANUFACTURERS

Baccarat
Muerthe, France. Most important contemporary maker of crystal. Founded 1764. Wide variety of products.
Trademark registered 1860, still in use. Label or acid etched:

George Bacchus & Son
Birmingham, England. Established c.1840. Influenced by Bohemian glass. Decorated opal ware, transfer printed with black, sepia and polychrome. Signature on vase, c.1850:

W. A. Bailey & Co.
London. Glass manufacturer. This trademark was registered and used from c.1908.

Dominik Bieman
(1800–1857), Frazenbad, Bohemia. Worked in Vienna and Prague. Engraved scenes and portraits. Many spellings of name.

DOMINIK BIEMANN

Boston & Sandwich Glass Company
Formerly the Sandwich Manufacturing Company. Established 1825 in Sandwich, Massachusetts by Deming Jarves, an agent of the New England Glass Company. Best known maker of American press-moulded glass (patent granted in 1827), also made lacy glass, and a huge variety of paperweights. Later incorporated into the New England Glass Company.

Philippe Brocard
France. Active from 1867, died 1896. Syrian-style decoration. Brocard et Fils (1884–1896).

Signature, gilt script on base of enamelled vase:

BROCARD/PARIS/1876

Signature, in gilt script:

Frederick Carder
(1867–1963) Designer with Steven & Williams, England, from 1880–1903. Moved to United States and made glass blanks for Hawkes Glass Works. Established Steuben Glass Works, Corning, New York. Signature used on cameo vase made while at Steven & Williams:

```
F. CARDER, S & W
F. CARDER 1897
```

Other signatures of various sizes and styles engraved with wheel on flexible shaft. May include a date:

F. Carder

```
"F. CARDER"
with fleur de lis
F. CARDER/AURENE/
STEUBEN
```

Louis Damon
France, died 1947. In 1900 won silver medal for carved vases. Retailer/designer, commissioned blanks from Daum (see *below*). Signature engraved on bottom of cameo vase:

Daum et Cie
Important glassworks in France. Established in 1875. During each period, Daum produced a wide range of styles. In 1969, began to make a series of limited edition plates.
Signature may be in enamel or cameo on side, or engraved with

gilt underfoot. Examples of signatures used until about 1895:

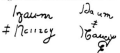

1895–1920:

George Davidson & Co.
England, established in 1867, quality pressed, slag and other domestic wares.
Signature moulded in ware:

Tradename used in the 1960s:

CHIPPENDALE

J. Derbyshire & Co.
(1856–1893), Manchester, England. Decorative wares.

Desprez
c.1790–1830, Paris. By 1819 making cameos embedded in crystal. Signature impressed on back of sulphide plaque, c.1800:

DESPREZ

DESPREZ /
RUE DES RÉCOLETS
NO. 2 A PARIS

Dorflinger Glass Works
White Mills, Pennsylvania. Active 1852–1921. Founded by Christian Dorflinger (1828–1915), born and trained in France. Maker of very fine cut and other glass.
Trademark:

Friedrich Egermann
(1777–1864) Born at Blottendorf, Bohemia. Established a workshop at Haida where he experimented with a variety of techniques. He patented *Lithyalin*, a marbled, opaque glass in 1828. Signatures on *Lithyalin* are rare and often obliterated. Egermann also discovered new methods of staining glass red and yellow.
Signature on enamelled beaker:

F. E.

Hieronimus William Fritchie
(1888–1916) Corning, New York, Toledo, Ohio and Philadelphia, Pennsylvania.
Signature in diamond point script on engraved glass:

H W FRITCHIE

Cristallerie d'Emile Gallé
Nancy, France. Emile Gallé (1846–1904), was a leader of the Art Nouveau movement. He established his own glass house for art glass in 1867. Used marquetry, cameo, engraving, and other techniques for vases, lamps and tableware. Clear enamelled items showing Islamic and Venetian influences. Best known for carved and etched glass. Most wares high quality, individually decorated. Also produced a commercial line of acid etched cameo for the popular market.
Engraved signature, with many other variations:

Signature on cameo with many other variations (*below left*):
A star beside name (see *below right*) denotes work produced after Gallé's death to represent the loss of one of France's shining stars. The star was used from September 1904 until 1914.

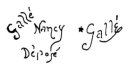

Mrs Graydon-Stannus
London, active 1923–1932. Maker of decorative wares using opal glass, clear glass with applied decoration, *Cluthra* and flashed glass. Forgeries are reported.

Henry Greener & Co.

Established 1858, Sunderland, England. Late 19thC. Lacy pressed (c.1870–1880), slag, commemoratives, etc. Mark used from 1884.

Signature moulded in pressed ware: mark *left* used 1875–1885; mark *right* used c.1885–1900. Continental copies are unmarked.

James Hateley

Birmingham, England. Trademark registered 1887!

Thomas G. Hawkes & Co.

Corning, New York. Trademark from 1902 for fine intaglio cut glass of the late brilliant period. Trademark acid etched, usually on centre-bottom, or on side of vessel. Beware of forgeries on wrong type of glass.

Registered trade name. Has been reported to be used as an acid stamp in block letters on wares other than Hawkes.

GRAVIC

A. H. Heisey & Co.

Newark, Ohio. Established 1893 by Major A. H. Heisey, closed in 1958. Used on cut glass, pressed glass, table and other wares. Trademark registered c.1900. Signature moulded in glass:

Moulded signature. Many fakes, some as recent as 1894. Check quality of glass and shape of diamond. Heisey now controls all moulds.

Imperial Russian Glass Manufactory.

Active during the reign of Tsar Nicholas II 1894–1917. Signature used on overlay vase with floral design, engraved under foot:

Lalique

René Lalique (1860–1945), French glassmaker and jewelry designer, famous for his scent bottles. The Lalique glassworks also produced glass screens, lamps, car mascots, fountains and lights. Usually worked with frosted white, opalescent glass and rarely used colour. Used naturalistic motifs for decoration, including fish, animals, flowers, leaves and fruit.

After his death his son Marc, continued the business as "Cristal Lalique", and modern pieces are marked "Lalique, France".

Engraved signature:

Lalique

Impressed mark:

[ALIQUE]

Lazarus and Isaac Jacobs

Father (died 1796) and son. In 1805 established Non-Such Flint Glass Manufactory, Bristol, and was glassmaker to George III. Signature in gilt on deep cobalt blue wares:

I. Jacobs Bristol   *I Jacobs Bristol*

Jefferson Glass Co.

Follansbee, West Virginia. Domestic and decorative wares. Trademark active 1907, label:

CHIPPENDALE

Trademark registered 1913, impressed on lighting wares:

Josephenenhütte, Gräfe
Schaffgotschische Glasfabrik in
Schrieberhau/Riesengeberge,
Germany.
Signature found on Biedermeier
beaker:

**Rheinische Glashütten, Köln
Ehrenfeld**
Germany, active 1864–1931.
Iridescent, Art Nouveau,
reproductions of 16th and
17thC designs, and tableware.
Trademarks *below* (mark, *right*,
found etched under foot of
covered pokal, c.1888):

W. L. Libbey & Son
Toledo, Ohio. Established 1893,
presently operating as division of
Ownes-Illinois. Makers of fine
glassware. Made brilliant cut
wares of fine quality during late
19thC, later used moulded
blanks. Produced Amberine,
Pomona, Maize, Peachblow, and
other art glass.
Mark used 1892–96, paper label
or printed in light reddish brown
on souvenirs:

1896–1906 etched on cut glass:

1919–1930:

J. & L. Lobmeyr
Signature engraved or enamelled.
Used after 1860:

Moncrieff's Glass Works
Perthshire, Scotland. John
Moncrieff, c.1922 began to make
decorative wares. "Monart" glass
was developed in 1924, by

Salvador Ysart (1887–1956). Made
only by him and his son, Paul.
The glass is clear, heavy, streaked
with black, scarlet and other Art
Deco colours. Also maker of
paperweights. Contemporary line
of art glass called "Monax".

Trademark on paper label. One
reference reports the original to
be green, another reports the
label as gold with black.

Mont Joye et Cie
Produced intaglio, cameo, or faux
cameo designs with enamels.
Landscape and floral subjects
were popular.
Signature acid-cut cameo design
and signature, sometimes with
enhancement; similar variations
on other wares:

J. Mortlock & Co.
London, England.
Trademark registered 1880:

Ludwig Moser & Söhne
Ludwig Moser (1833–1916), glass
engraver and merchant. Trained
at Karlsbad (Karlovy Vary),
Bohemia (now Czech Republic)
in the school that formed around
master engraver Andreas Mattoni.
Active from 1857 onwards.
Established a factory at
Meierhöfen (Nové Dvory),
c.1857. Wares included cameo-
carved cased glass. In 1970,
introduced limited edition
copper-wheel engraved plates.
Engraved on side:

MOSER
Moser
Karlsbad

Mount Washington Glass Co.
South Boston, Massachusetts. Established 1837, resumed original name 1871. Acquired by Pairpoint, c.1894. Mould blown and pressed art glass: "Burmese", "Royal Flemish", cut glass etc. Trademark: original is a paper label. Forgeries made of same form are acid etched. "Royal Flemish" ware gives an appearance of stained glass sections separated by raised gilt lines.

Müller Frères
Established c.1910 near Lunéville (Lorraine), France, by Henri Müller and his brother, Désiré, when joined with the glassworks established c.1900 by Henri Müller at Croismare. Art glass of many different types. Signature cameo on four-layer, four-acid-cut cameo vase:

"Luneville" added after 1910. Mark *below* engraved on side. "Crosimare" added after 1900; signed in red under foot:

Follett & Clarkson Osler
Birmingham, England. Established 1807. Signature moulded in frosted solid glass bust portraits:

    F & C OSLER /
    1 MAY 1845

Gebrüder Pallme-König
Steinschönau, Czechoslovakia. Established in 1786. Art glass. Signature on paper label printed black on gold applied to Art Deco perfume bottles early 20thC:

Pilkington Bros. Ltd.
St. Helens, England. Established 1826; later changed to Pilkington Glass Manufacturing Co., England & Canada. Decorative and domestic wares. Trademark registered 1877, printed or moulded:

W. H., B. & J. Richardson
Wordsley, England. c.1836–c.1850 when it became Henry G. Richardson & Sons (see *below*). Signature: enamel decoration and signature. Early decorations were black; later polychrome. One piece of each set was signed:

    RICHARDSON'S VITRIFIED

    RICHARDSON'S VIRTIFIED
    ENAMEL COLOURS

Signed on vessel with classical figures painted in iron red:

    RICHARDSON'S STOURBRIDGE

Henry G. Richardson & Sons
Wordsley, England. Sold to Thomas Webb about 1930. Trademark, registration date not known:

Compagnie des Cristalleries de St. Louis
Münzthal, Lorraine. Wide range of fine crystal items made up to present day. Trademark:

Signature c.1871–1918:

    ST LOUIS - MUNZTHAL

Etched on cameo vase:

    ST LOUIS, NANCY

Cross of Lorraine appears in various locations, either over or under the tail of the "L":

Sowerby & Neville (1855–5720); Sowerby & Co. (1872–1881); Sowerby Ellison Glassworks (1881–).
Gateshead-on-Tyne, England. Inexpensive pressed, slag, spangled, etc. Marked from 1876 onwards.
Signature moulded in ware, usually under base, sometimes in interior. May also have registry mark.

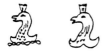

Steuben Glass Works
Established 1903 by Frederick Carder in Corning, New York. Taken over by Corning Glass Works in 1918. Mark 1903–1932 was acid-stamped fleur-de-lys with "Steuben" on a scroll. Mark after 1932:

Stevens & Williams.
England, 19thC makers of art glass.
Signature in cameo on acid cut-back vase, at bottom:

Trade name etched on cover of lead crystal jar, 20thC:

Etched in yellow under base of vase, c.1928. Trademark registered in 1926. Royal warrant received in 1919.

Strathearn Glass Co., Vasart Glass Ltd
Scotland. Hand-blown vases of mottled colours, *Clutha*, etc. Trade name active 1970s.
Signature on base of vessel with rough wheel engraving:

Tiffany Furnaces
Corona, N.Y. Trademark registered 1902, used only as a label. Never etched on glass wares:

Patented 1912. Trade name not used as a permanent mark on *Fabrique* glass panels in lamp shades.

Favrile fabrique

Tiffany Glass and Decorating Co.
New York, N.Y. 1892–1902. Established by Louis Comfort Tiffany. Leaded windows, art glass lamps and vases.
Trademark issued 13 November 1894, used as a paper label embossed in green and gold, or printed in black and white. May read *Favrile* or *Fabrile*. Printed labels may have glass type between *Favrile* and *Glass* – for example, "Sunset". This monogram was not used as an etched signature:

Tiffany Glass Co.
1886–92, rare signature may be acid stamped in pontil. Beware of forgeries:

Tiffany Studios
Formerly the Tiffany Glass and Decorating Co. (see *above*), New York, N.Y. Trademark registered c.1904, but in use after 1902. Undertook interior design commissions, and expanded to make a wide range of items in many different materials, including glass, using innovative techniques. Studios closed after Tiffany's death in 1933.
Paper label, not an acid stamp:

Tiffany & Co.
New York, N.Y. Retail jewelers, established 1834 by Tiffany's father Charles Lewis Tiffany. Mark used on wares from numerous sources retailed in the New York store:

Cristalleries du Val-St.-Lambert
Liège, Belgium. Established 1825, still largest glassworks in Belgium. Art glass and fine useful wares.
Trademark acid etched on Art Deco vase, c.1920:

Signature, a wide variety of styles:

E. Varnish & Co.
London, England. Licensee of F. Hale Thonson's patent of 1849 for double-walled glassware, the interior walls lined with silver. Signature impressed on the plug for the hole that seals the silver:

E. VARNISH & CO.

Waterford
Waterford Glass House, established by George and William Penrose, first mentioned in 1783. Marked pieces include decanters, finger-bowls and jugs.

Waterford Crystal Ltd
Waterford, Ireland. Opened 1851, Maker of good quality stemware, lamps, etc
Trademark:

Signature in block or gothic letters etched on base of items:

Waterloo Co.
Cork, Ireland, c.1815. Decanters. Signature moulded in base:

WATERLOO CO / CORK

Thomas Webb & Sons
John Shepherd & Thos. Webb at White House Glass Works 1833–1840; Thos. Webb's glassworks "The Flats" 1840–1855; Thos. Webb, Dennis Glass Works, 1835–1859; Thos. Webb & Sons, Dennis Glass Works, 1859 onwards.
Signature engraved on cameo work:

THOS. WEBB & SON

Acid etched on Burmese Ware:

Other signatures on cameo pieces:

THOMAS WEBB & SONS/

THOS. WEBB & SONS

Thomas and George Woodall
England, established by brothers Thomas (1849–1926) and George (1850–1925). Cameo carvers, worked at Thomas Webb & Sons. Signature 1880–1900:

J & G Woodall

BIBLIOGRAPHY

Battie, David and Cottle, Simon (Eds.), *Sotheby's Concise Encyclopedia of Glass*, London, 1991

Beck, Doreen, *The Book of Bottle Collecting*, Middlesex, 1973

Bickerton, L. M., *Eighteenth Century English Drinking Glasses: An Illustrated Guide*, Suffolk, 1986

Bickerton, L. M., *English Drinking Glasses 1675–1825*, Buckinghamshire, 1987

Bly, John (Ed.), *Is it Genuine? How to Collect Antiques With Confidence*, London, 1986

Davis, Derek C. *English Bottles & Decanters 1650–1900*, London 1972

Davis, Derek C., *Glass for Collectors*, London, 1971

Drahotová, Olga, *European Glass*, London, 1983

Gibbs-Smith, C. H., *The Great Exhibition of 1851*, London, 1981

Haslam, Malcolm, *Arts & Crafts: A Buyer's Guide to the Decorative Arts in Britain and America 1860–1930*, London, 1988

Haslam, Malcolm, *Art Nouveau: A Buyer's Guide to the Decorative Arts of the 1900s*, London, 1988

Haynes, E. Barrington, *Glass Through the Ages*, Middlesex, 1970

Hollingworth, Jane, *Collecting Decanters*, London, 1980

Hughes, Therle, *The Country Life Antiques Handbook*, London, 1986

Jervis, Simon, *The Penguin Dictionary of Design and Designers*, London, 1984

Klein, Dan and Lloyd, Ward (Eds.), *The History of Glass*, London, 1984

Knowles, Eric, *Victoriana to Art Deco*, London, 1992

Lattimore, Colin R., *English 19thC Press-Moulded Glass*, London, 1979

Miller's *Antiques & Collectables: The Facts at Your Fingertips*, London, 1993

Miller's Antiques Checklist: *Art Deco*, London, 1991

Miller's Antiques Checklist: *Art Nouveau*, London, 1992

Miller's Antiques Checklist: *Victoriana*, London, 1991

Miller, Judith and Martin, *Understanding Antiques*, London, 1989

Miller, Muriel M., *Glass*, Middlesex, 1990

Osbourne, Harold (Ed.),*The Oxford Companion to the Decorative Arts*, Oxford, 1985

Phillips, Phoebe (Ed.), *The Encyclopedia of Glass*, London, 1981

Porter, Norman and Jackson, Douglas, *Tiffany Glassware*, London, 1988

Savage, George, *Dictionary of Antiques*, London, 1978

Slack, Raymond, *English Pressed Glass, 1830–1900*, London, 1987

Smith, John P. *Osler's Crystal for Royalty and Rajahs*, London, 1991

The Collector's Encyclopedia, *Victoriana to Art Deco*, London, 1980

INDEX

PICTURE CREDITS AND ACKNOWLEDGEMENTS

The publishers would like to thank the following auction houses, museums, dealers and other sources for supplying pictures for use in this book, or for allowing their pieces to be photographed.

1 IB/MW; **3** SL; **16** SL; **18** CL; **19** all CL; **20** CL; **21** all CL; **22** SL; **24** tCL, bCL; **25** all CL; **26** all CL; **27** trSL, clSL, brIB/MW; **28** tSL; **29** all SL; **30** SL; **32** SL; **33** tlSL; crSL, blIB/MW; **34** IB/MW; **35** tl SA, tc IB/MW, tr IB/MW, brIB/MW; **36** SL; **37** trSL, clCL, brCL; **38** CL; **39** all SL; **40** SL; **41** trCL, clSL, brCL; **42** SL; **43** tSL, brIB/MW; **44** SL; **45** trIB/MW, clSL, br IB/MW; **46** SL; **47** trIB/MW, blSL; **48** IB/MW; **50** SL; **51** all IB/MW; **52** SL; **53** trIB/MW, clSL, br IB/MW; **54** SL; **55** all IB/MW; **56** SL; **57** all SL; **58** SL; **59** trSL, blCL, brCL; **60** CNY; **62** tCMG, bPC; **63** trIB/MW, brPC; **64**CNY; **65** all CNY; **66** all IB/MW; **67** lSNY, rIB/MW; **68** SNY; **70** SL; **71** tCL, blIB/MW, brIB/MW; **72** SL; **73** trCL, blSL, brSL; **74** IB/MW; **75** tlPC, crV&A; **76** rIB/MW, brSNY; **77** all SHK; **78** M; **80** SL; **81** all SL; **82** M; **83** trSL, clSL, brCL; **84** SL; **85** tlSL, crSL, bIB/MW; **86** SL; **87** trIB/MW, clS; **88** IB/MW; **89** all IB/MW; **90** SL; **91** all IB/MW; **92** IB/MW; **93** tlIB/MW, crIB/MW, blSL; **94** IB/MW; **95** tlIB/MW, crIB/MW, blSL; **96** SL; **97** tlIB/MW, crCL, blIB/MW; **98** CL; **99** tlCL, trCL, brSL; **100** IB/MW; **101** all IB/MW; **104** SL; **106** CL; **107** lCL, rSL; **108** IB/MW; **109** all IB/MW; **110** IB/MW; **111** all IB/MW; **112** SL; **113** all IB/MW; **114** IB/MW; **115** all IB/MW; **116** IB/MW; **117** all IB/MW; **118** IB/MW; **119** tlIB/MW, trIB/MW, blSC; **120** IB/MW; **121** tlIB/MW, trIB/MW, blIB/MW, brPL; **122** IB/MW; **123** tlWGT, blSL; **124** IB/MW; **125** tlIB/MW, crIB/MW, blIB/MW; **128** MW; **130** SL; **131** all IB/MW; **132** SL; **133** all IB/MW; **134** IB/MW; **135** all IB/MW; **136** IB/MW; **137** all IB/MW; **138** SL; **140** SL; **141** tlSL, crIB/MW, blIB/MW; **142** SL; **143** trCL, clSL, brCB; **144** CL; **145** trCL, clCL, brSL; **146** IB/MW; **148** CL; **149** all IB/MW; **150** IB/MW; **151** all IB/MW; **152** IB/MW; **153** all IB/MW; **154** all IB/MW; **155** all IB/MW; **156** IB/MW; **157** tlIB/MW, trIB/MW, cl IB/MW, crSL; **158** SL; **159** tlIB/MW, trIB/MW, blIB/MW, brM; **160** IB/MW; **161** all IB/MW; **162** IB/MW; **163** tlIB/MW, crIB/MW, bMB; **164** IB/MW; **165** all IB/MW; **166** IB/MW; **167** all IB/MW; **168** SL; **169** clSL, crIB/MW, blSL; **170** PC; **171** clH&G, bRS; **172** IB/MW; **173** all IB/MW; **174** SL; **175** all IB/MW

Key
b bottom, c centre, l left, r right, t top

CB	Christine Bridge Antiques, London		Mallett & Son (Antiques) Limited
CL	Christie's, London	MW	Photograph provided by Mark West
CMG	Picture reproduced with kind permission of the Corning Museum of Glass, Corning, New York	PC	Private Collection
		RS	Picture reproduced with kind permission of Raymond M. Slack F.R.S.A.
CNY	Christie's, New York	SA	Sotheby's, Amsterdam
H&G	Picture reproduced with kind permission of Hope & Glory, Kensington Church Street, London	SC	Sotheby's, Colonnade
		SHK	Sotheby's, Hong Kong
		SL	Sotheby's, London
		SNY	Sotheby's, New York
IB/MW	Photograph by permission of Mark West taken by Ian Booth on behalf of Reed Consumer Books	V&A	Picture reproduced with kind permission of the Victoria and Albert Museum, London
M	Picture reproduced with kind permission of	WGT	Picture reproduced with kind permission of W. G. T. Burne